Diego Esteban *Julio Cabos*

The Master painters Julio Cabos and Diego Esteban will guide us through the Warlord Saga world in order to help us explore it using their most useful painting fantasy figures techniques.

Julio Cabos, is the Master Painter of Andrea Miniatures and the author of several books on figure painting such as “Painting Figures with Acrylics” and “Painting Pin Up figures”, both of them published by Andrea Press.

During his career as a professional painter, he has worked in all kinds of projects accomplishing great results and receiving international awards. Thanks to these experiences he has become one of the most versatile and successful figure painters, with a great acceptance among professionals and amateurs in this hobby.

Diego Esteban is a young painter who has been, for nearly 10 years, working as a professional freelance painter. He has participated in national and international competitions, where he has been awarded in the top categories. At the age of 21, he studied illustration as a hobby. This helped him to complete many of his projects, using techniques such as composition, color and lighting.

WARLORD SAGA

Painting Gold Medal Fantasy Figures

Julio Cabos
Diego Esteban

A COMPLETE GUIDE FOR BASIC TO ADVANCED PAINTERS

ANDREA PRESS

Introduction

by José Manuel Palomares

Ancient shadows of the past are advancing, sinister and menacing. Two archaic demons are about to be released after centuries of being contained by powerful mystical seals.

Old warlords invoke old alliances and young warriors with a thirst for glory lead armies to meet their destiny.

Past quarrels are mixed with new moves for power on the old continent. While Beelphegor is breaking the seals, Zwëothel increases the armies of the undead. The arcane and the Edge of Amber, have begun to move their own threads, and Leogante has been called. Powerful warriors are becoming the keys to an uncertain destiny, while epic battles are being played on a huge chessboard.

In this fantasy figure painting monograph we will delve into the fascinating world of the Warlord Saga through some of its characters, learning from basic painting techniques to the most elaborated ones, guided by two Master painters who will teach us their working methods. Many of these painting techniques, such as the non-metallic metals (NMM) one, were developed years ago by renowned wargame figure painters. Our master painters will teach you both airbrush and paintbrush techniques applied to different processes. The use of the airbrush for painting figures, has contributed to the development of new approaches to fantasy painting, changing the classical concept.

You will also find fundamental for beginner painters such as how to choose the most appropriate highlighting for your miniature, how to paint eyes to give expression to the figure and so on.

You will find all of this and much more through detailed step by step processes, culminating with the painting process of a very special piece Beelphegor, Fire Wings (WSS-03).

Welcome to the Warlord Saga world

2

Materials for the preparation of a figure

All metal or resin figures require a simple and necessary preparation process before starting to paint them. While the parts are prepared, they can be studied and checked for flaws, facilitating the painting to obtain the best final results.

Files

They are necessary to eliminate the mold lines and leave surfaces clean of any manufacturing defect.

Blade with handle

Needed to cut, clean, or eliminate metal or resin parts, it is possibly one of the most important tools used for almost everything, both in the preparation of the figures and during the painting process for cutting and adjusting the adhesive masks.

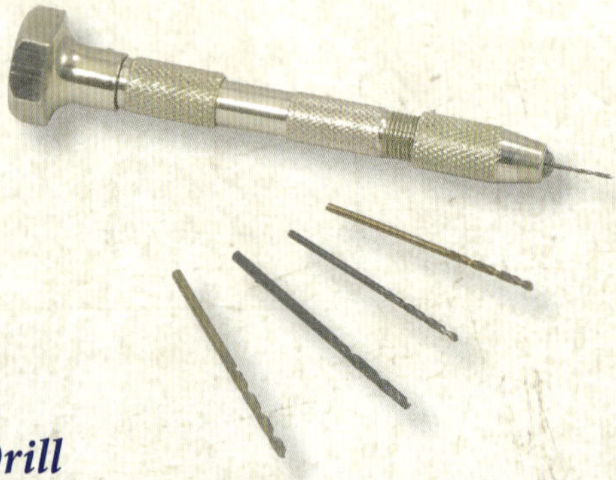

Drill

It is mainly used to make small holes where you can insert a metal pin, to secure and strengthen the details on those pieces that need to be reinforced due to their size or weight.

Sandpaper

Its use is essential to eliminate possible impurities from the metal and remove mold lines that have not been accessed with files. The different types of grits that can be employed range from 500 to 1000, leaving the latter for finer polishing.

Cutting pliers

When you attempt to cut the part from its metal matrix or other material, this tool is more effective than a blade, and above all, more secure.

Needle-nosed tweezers

Such tools are very practical for holding or bending small pieces. They are almost essential for holding very small pieces and attaching them to another part of the figure.

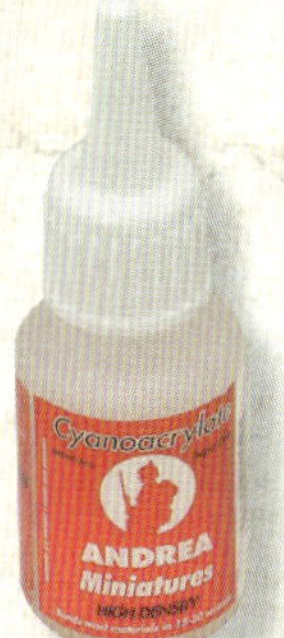

Cyanoacrylate adhesive

This product is ideal for very small parts that are not well attached. Only a small drop of glue is necessary and it is advisable that sticking points be clean of any traces of paint or other waste materials.

Cyanoacrylate accelerator

It is applied onto the part where you just put a drop of glue, accelerating the bonding process instantly. This product is ideal for application on those parts which are very small and their union is tiny and they are not well fastened.

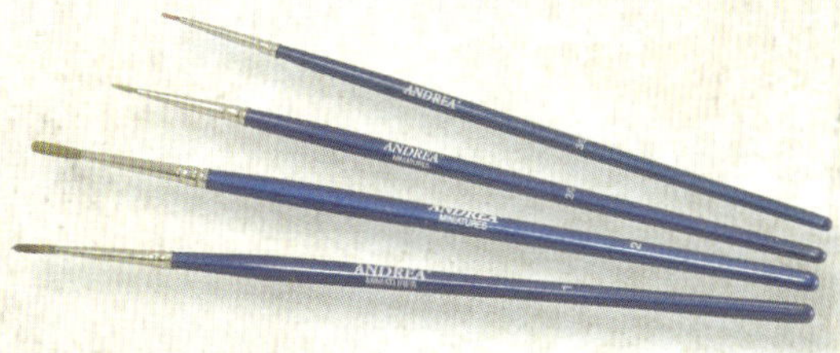

Synthetic brushes

These are brushes that also serve to sculpt, giving the desired shape to the putty. The hardness of the fibers allows you to work the putty better.

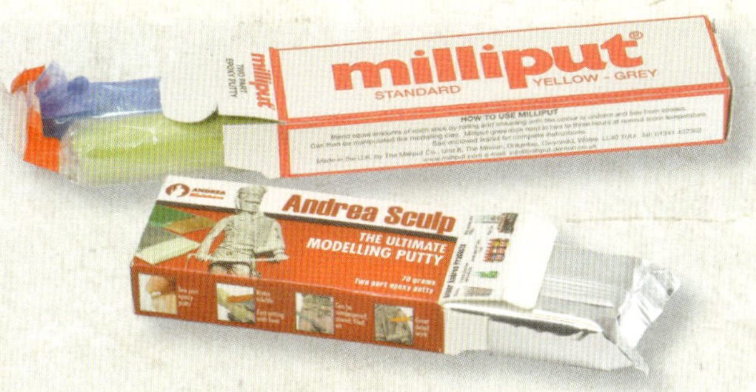

Two-component putty

It is used by mixing the two components in equal parts until you get a uniform color of the mass. It is easily malleable and drying times range from 30 minutes to an hour, although it can be accelerated by application of heat.

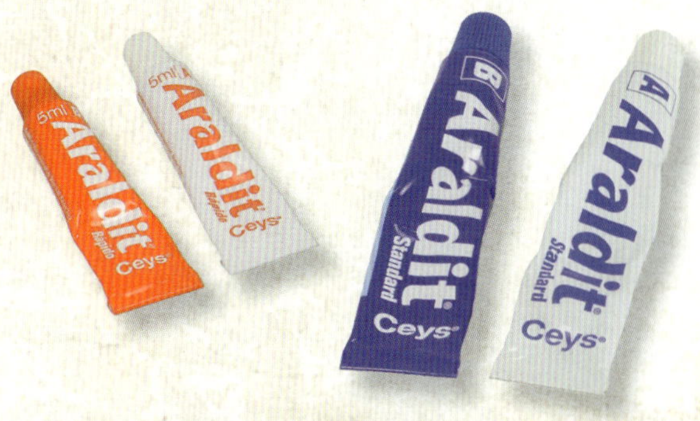

Two-component glue

This type of glue is used to attach large items or those that weigh a lot, allowing for a stronger grip. The two parts are mixed to fifty percent each, and it has a maximum working time of 5 to 10 minutes until it finishes drying completely.

Spatulas for modeling

Such tools are essential when applying material and giving shape to the putty or modeling paste. Many of these tools are made or handcrafted by modelers themselves.

Primer spray

It is the other alternative to the airbrush for priming figures. It is best to spray the top layers at a distance of between 15cm to 20cm with short sprays. Let the model dry between applications. Never leave the Jet of paint fixed on a point on the model to avoid build-up that hides details.

Preparation of a figure

The preparation of a figure is mostly the removal of mold production lines and bonding of those parts whose attachment is essential before tackling the paint job.

To delete seam lines, in metal or resin, first use in round or half round files. To complete the task and leave the smoother surface, you can use medium grit (600) sandpaper and go through other finer grits to obtain an absolutely polished surface.

The glue we use to attach most of the pieces is cyanoacrylate. We must be careful that it does not overflow edges at joints, since once it dries, that excess will leave a visible layer of adhesive that will not only increase visually when we paint the figure, but can cover any fine detail. In this case, we must remove the excess with very fine sandpaper to leave the area completely clean.

Sometimes the connection of some glued parts is still visible. To address this point, we will use two-component putty. Once the two parts (putty and hardener) are mixed with a thin spatula and synthetic brushes soaked in water, we spread the putty, shaping it as needed to leave the seam fully sealed. If necessary, sand the putty, but this should only be done once it is completely dry.

In some cases, reconstruction can be a bit more complex and we will need to mimic the original textures to integrate the joining of parts, and to choose the most suitable tool for this task.

The last step is to the prime the whole figure. This not only will not help our paint to adhere better but it makes the colors look more intense, and we can verify that setting and application of the putty in the joints are perfect.

1

2

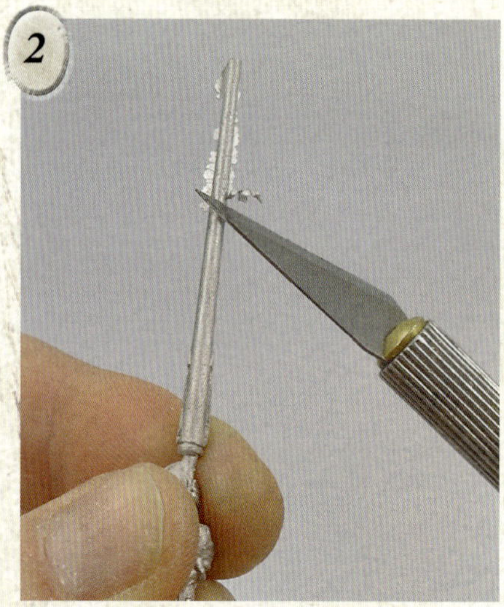

3

1. Use cutting pliers to remove parts from the mold sprues.

2. To remove metal burrs, use a blade with a handle.

3. Round files are the most suitable to remove the mold parting lines.

4. Usually cyanoacrylate glue is used, especially if the pieces are resin, like in this case.

5. Fill the joints between the parts with two-component putty. We do it with the help of synthetic brushes soaked in water or with spatulas.

6. If it is necessary to integrate the texture of putty with the rest of the piece, is made with fresh paste. In this case a hypodermic needle was used to mimic the texture of the skin.

Priming the figure is an essential step before beginning to paint.

Paints and materials

There are many different materials that can be used to paint figures. The choice of materials can make a big difference in the outcome of our work without being an expert connoisseur of various painting techniques. The paints which were used to paint the figures in this book are intended and designed especially for this function, although they can also be used for other artwork such as painting on paper or on other media.

Andrea Color Paint Sets (ACS)

This is a set of specific colors with six bottles of paint, to allow you to quickly and simply paint the full figure starting with: base color, two or three highlights, as well as shadows. They are compatible with the general range as they can be used with brush and airbrush. (See color chart).

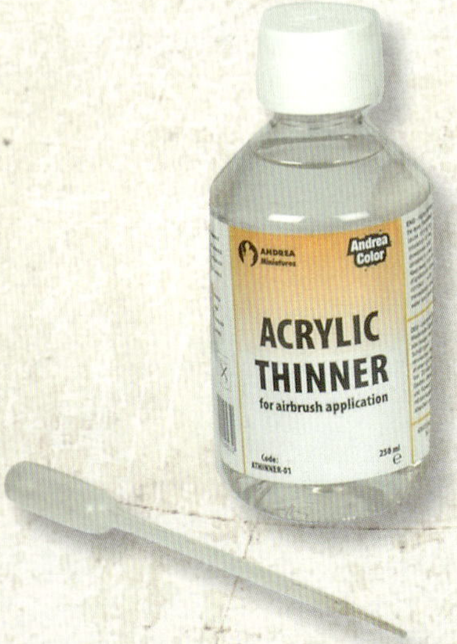

Acrylic thinner (Athinner - 01)

This thinner is specifically designed to be used with acrylic paints XNAC and ACS if you are going to paint with airbrush. Add a few drops of thinner to the cup of the airbrush and mix it with paint, checking to see if the mix is suitable for the work we are going to do.

Color palettes

We can find different models that fit our needs. Even though many painters prefer a plastic or similar plate, there are other options.

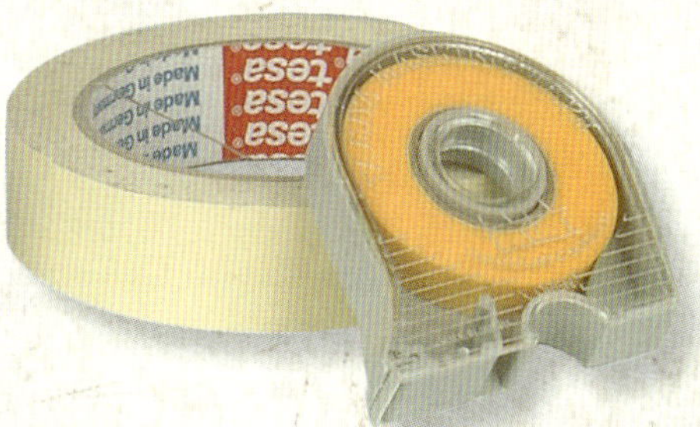

Adhesive tape

This material is essential when painting with an airbrush. There are different types and thicknesses, but it is always advisable to use those which are recommended for airbrushing work.

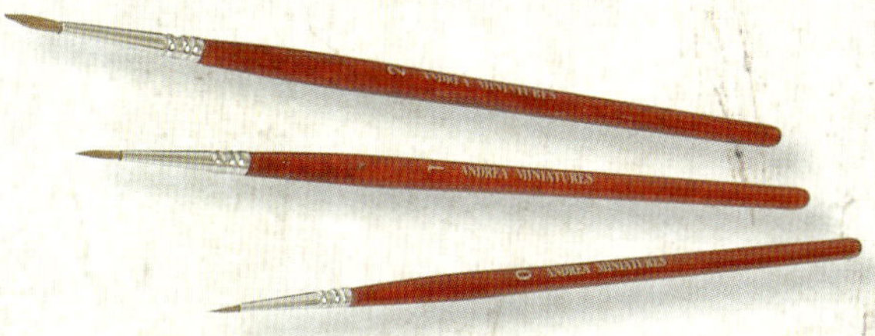

Kolinsky hair brushes (KS-0, KS-1 and KS-2)

They are perfect for figure painting, since their smoothness and fine tip allow us to perform all kinds of work. It is important to keep your tip in good condition, clean it thoroughly with soap and water when you are done with your painting session.

Acrylic colors Andrea Color (XNAC)

It consists of 60 colors that are compatible for use with brush and airbrush. (See color chart).

Compressor and airbrush

The compressor is the power supply of the airbrush, which is necessary to keep a constant pressure, so that you air flow is never uncontrolled while you're painting. There is a wide variety of airbrush models in the market with multiple functions, but the most versatile is the double action with the connector integrated into the airbrush body. The size of the needle can vary according to manufacturer from 0, 2 mm, 3 mm to 4 mm.

3.1

Basic painting

by Julio Cabos

To get a perfect gradation of colors applied to a figure, it is necessary to first paint on a uniform base color, without covering the fine detail. To this base color is added a fraction of one or several lighter colors, making a new mixture slightly more liquid to allow for a somewhat transparent and fluid brushwork. This second mix which is referred to as a rising highlight, should not completely cover the base color. In the same way, but on the contrary, if we add a darker color to the base color, which is called a shadow, you will have the same treatment as with the highlight.

We can work with two types of palettes that are commonly used for acrylic paints: the traditional one and the wet one.

The traditional palette for acrylic paint is usually made of plastic or metal and allows us to make several mixtures of paint at the same time on the same surface, without mixing them randomly. Another advantage is that having a greater amount of paint makes easier to use it with an airbrush. The problem normally arising from this type of palette is that in certain environmental conditions (excess of heat or low humidity) the paint dries quickly. If we see that our painting day is over and we want to preserve the fresh mixtures, we just need to place the palette in the freezer.

On the other hand, the wet palette always keeps the colors and mixtures wet, so it is easier to control the amount of water, the colors' dilution and their mixtures throughout the painting process. The main disadvantage of this type of palette is that it is more complicated to make as many mixtures as you can create with the traditional one, unless they are mixed with other colors.

1

2

3

4

TRADITIONAL PALETTE

1. *Materials.*

WET PALETTE

2. *Materials.*

3. *Plastic plate.*

4. *Paper towel placement.*

5. *Add water.*

6. *Baking paper placement.*

7. *Paint mixture.*

Now, how are the highlights and the shadows applied?

We should choose which will be our main point of light for the whole figure. The most used light scheme in painting figures has been the zenithal one. It is the light that is projected on our figure from above. If we imagine that we have primed the figure under a hose, and seeing where the areas of light, shadows and even some intermediate areas of lights and shadows are shown.

But you can also choose other points of light that are not from the top-down, even a directional light approach can be great. In this way the light that illuminates the figure can come from one side, more or less from above, or even from a light bulb held by the figure itself.

Zenithal light

To follow the scheme of zenithal lighting, we must study the volumes of the figure and see how light behaves on them. For example, as I explained previously imagine your figure placed under a hose for priming. Your brush must continue with its tipped a little to cover a larger surface area, thus the brushstroke will leave more paint at the point where it is separated from the surface. Following this system, if we are working on highlights, the direction of the stroke will be extended from the area where light first appears to the point of maximum light. In the case of the shadows, it will be the opposite. The line will extend from area where shadow begins towards the zone of maximum darkness. If during the process of highlighting and shadowing you find an unwanted stroke, you only need to add a little more water to the mixture and apply an intermediate layer.

There is a final concept of blending between maximum light levels and maximum shadow. They are the values half-light and half dark, also termed intermediate tones. These tones are applied through thin glazes where you never try to cover the color that precedes it, but to overlap the layers with a varying color, without losing the essence of previous processes.

1. *Base applied in two coats of paint, letting the first dry before applying the next one.*

2. *First light, with this first mix, several layers are applied on areas for illumination, since the mixture is slightly more diluted than the base color.*

3. *Second light, the brushstroke will cut gradually towards the area that receives more light.*

4. *Third light focuses only on the points where the light falls with maximum intensity.*

5. *First shadow, where the brush stroke is opposite to that of the highlights.*

6. *Apply an intermediate tone on some of the areas between the highlight and the base color, enriching the previous processes.*

7. *Another intermediate tone, this time on the areas between the shade and the base color.*

3 LIGHT	2 LIGHT	1 LIGHT	BASE	1 SHADOW	MIDTONES
XNAC 43 + XNAC 45 + ACS 01: Nº4	1 LIGHT + XNAC 43	BASE + XNAC 43	ACS 01: Nº4 + XNAC 05 + XNAC 31 + XNAC 49	BASE + XNAC 11 + XNAC 45 + XNAC 32	BASE + XNAC 45 + 11 BASE + ACS 01: Nº2 + ACS 03: Nº1

Directed light

This scheme of light requires a color palette with somewhat more elaborate preparation, where two different base colors, one for the more illuminated area and another for the darker area, will be used. In the same way, each part will need its own corresponding highlights and shadows.

A tool that can help us with the first steps of the development of this effort is the airbrush. With it we can project the direction of the light with paint, and create a subtle but at the same time well differentiated transition between both zones.

After this first phase, we go to the brush to define and highlight the finer details. To achieve a perfect combination of both techniques, one of the keys is the way of applying brushstrokes, to avoid losing some of the previous process and at the same time enhance those points, it is essential to work with them with a brush. To achieve this, we must only follow the advice explained in the previous section, where the inclination of the brush along the direction of the stroke will give us the results we seek.

1. Paint the base color with your airbrush on the lightest part of the face. As you can see, we arrange the figure so as to concentrate the paint from below the face and fading towards the top.

2. Repeat the same process with a darker color mixing base, but to the opposite side of the face.

3. Front view of this first step completed with an airbrush.

4. First highlight on the lightest part of the face.

5. First highlight on the dark part of the face.

6. First shadow on the light side of the face.

7. First shadow on the other side of the face.

2 LIGHT	1 LIGHT	BASE	1 SHADOW	
XNAC 01 + XNAC 43 + XNAC 17	BASE + XNAC 01 + XNAC 17	XNAC 45 + XNAC 31 + XNAC 01 + XNAC 17	BASE + XNAC 29 + XNAC 50 +	A side of the face

8. *Apply a second highlight that will only be on this side of the face to accentuate the effect of directed lighting.*

9. *On the dark side, only apply a second shadow, to enhance the contrast on the lighter side.*

10. *Final view of the process.*

1 LIGHT	BASE	1 SHADOW	2 SHADOW
BASE + XNAC 31	BASE light side + XNAC 48 + ACS 02: Nº5	BASE + XNAC 29 +	1 SHADOW + XNAC 30 + XNAC 50

The dark side of the face

Other examples of directed light

Daramis, Healing Light
WS-28

Olfo, "Fast feet"
WS-25

4

Painting the eyes

by Julio Cabos

Altogether, a figure's face is the part that most arouses the viewer's attention. The eyes are, at the same time, the focus within the face. Through them, the figure conveys the attitude or the nature of his character. Because of that, it is very important to know how to properly choose the direction of the gaze and even the eye color that best fits the character.

In this case, it's a dwarf in a relaxed pose looking at the smoke wafting from the pipe that he holds in his left hand. This could be one of the possible options for painting the eyes and perhaps the most successful, although they also could look in other directions. Given the size of the figure, the ideal brush would a number 0 or 1, whichever one of yours has a tip in perfect condition. If the figure is primed gray, we start by painting the eyeball in an off-white color. If the primer is white it is not necessary to do this step. We load the brush with a very smooth dark brown mix by adjusting the load of paint by removing the excess on absorbent paper. It is now time to mark the line of the upper eyelash along the upper eyelid. Do the same with the lower eyelid with a lighter reddish brown.

Finally put in the iris and, within this, the pupil. With a figure of this scale, you can paint some reflections within the iris giving it a more realistic finish, although it is more important to keep the eyes' size and shape right, than to try to recreate these details on a badly painted eye.

1. The eyeball is painted in off-white, and outlined with dark brown upper eyelids.

2. With a tone of light reddish brown, outline the lower eyelids.

3. Use a "marta kolinsky" hair brush of Number 1 or 0 to paint the iris. Is it possible that during this process will have to make some changes to the off-white color to give the iris its correct size and shape.

4. Lighten the center of the iris without reaching the edges of the same.

5. Paint the pupil in matte black.

6. The final touch is a fine dot of matte white, between the iris and the pupil to give a more realistic effect.

Painting hair and beard

by Julio Cabos

Let's look at two examples on this same miniature where we had previously painted the skin with a zenithal light from above and the other with a directional light. In each case regardless of the color you choose, development of the highlights and shadows of the hair and the beard will be affected by the type of lighting hitting each example. In both cases will use only the brush.

White hair and beard

The approach of this figure is designed with an overhead zenithal light, and we will begin applying a base color equally to all parts. We continue with the highlights which will be distributed over the areas impacted by direct light, forgetting the finer details of the hair, i.e. we are going to paint from the general to the specific. As we move forward with the second and third highlights, we can define some details of the modeling of the hair and beard in a more particular way. The process of shadows is the same as that of the highlights, only that it is not necessary to give more than two shades to achieve the desired finish.

1. Base color of the hair and beard, applied in two coats of paint.

2. The first highlight is painted on the spots where the Zenithal light falls directly on the hair and the beard, ignoring the finer details of the sculpture.

3. For the second highlight, brush strokes are added to areas of maximum light, concentrating on the finer details of the sculpture.

4-5. For the third and last highlight, touches with the brush are only applied on the points of maximum highlight accentuating the most delicate details of beard and hair.

6. *We will give the first shadow the same treatment we used for the first highlight.*

7. *With the second shadow, emphasize those parts where light has less impact.*

8. *Apply an intermediate shade between the highlight and shadow levels.*

3 LIGHT	2 LIGHT	1 LIGHT	BASE COLOR	1 SHADOW	2 SHADOW	MIDTONE
ACS 03: Nº4	ACS 03: Nº3	ACS 03: Nº 2	ACS 03: Nº1 + ACS 03: Nº6	ACS 03: Nº6	ACS 03:Nº6+ ACS 12:Nº5	1 SHADOW + XNAC 40

5.2

Red hair and beard

This other example has a type of directional lighting, which must be repeated on all parts of the figure, otherwise we will see an inconsistency in the lighting scheme, completely losing the initial effect. For this purpose, we must prepare two different base color tones; one for the dark part, and one for the lightest area. Different processes of highlights and shadows corresponding to each area must be applied in the same way. What will not change is the way we add highlights and shadows which will be like the previous example, from the general to the specific.

1. *Base color of the hair and beard corresponding to the lightest part of the head.*

2. *Base color of the darker area.*

2 LIGHT	1 LIGHT	BASE
ACS 04: Nº 4 + XNAC 35 + XNAC 17	ACS 04.Nº 1 + XNAC 35	ACS 04: Nº1 + ACS 04: Nº4 + XNAC 47

A side of the face

3

4

5

6

7

3. First highlight on the light base color of the hair and beard.

4. First highlight on the dark base color.

5. Apply a second highlight, only in the lightest area, to enhance the effect of directed light.

6. On the contrary, in the darkest area, apply only a second shadow.

7. Final view of the process.

1 LIGHT	BASE	SHADOW	
ACS 04: Nº 1 +	ACS 04:Nº 6 +	ACS 04: Nº6 + ACS 05: Nº6 +	Dark side

Another example of beard with directed light

Drünegar, The RuneKeeper
WS-03

6

Painting fabrics

by Diego Esteban

To get a seamless transition of the base color to the highlights and shadows in a fabric using the brush, is a challenge, especially when we are taking the first steps and the surface to paint has some volume. The brush is our best ally to give personality to our figures. With it, with him we can see that each brushstroke is unique, but we follow a certain method or system of common work.

We have chosen the set of red which, like the rest of the paint sets, is very practical in any case, but even more so for a novice painter, because when it comes to mixtures, the highlights and the shadows are simpler. The figure that we have chosen for teaching how to paint fabric is Zwëothel (WS-31). Since we want to achieve a bright color, it is important for us to prime the figure in white. Black Primer, by contrast, is often used to achieve a darker effect.

First we apply the base color in a uniform way.

We should previously have thought about the type of lighting that we want for our figure. The type of lighting with which we will work is overhead.

The next step is to illuminate, focusing mainly on the upper part of the folds, where more light is projected.

We will add a first extensive shadow partly opposite to the light of the folds. Then we apply a second highlight in a more specific area, e.g. on levels where the light falls more directly and reinforces the effect we want to achieve. And again, just as we have completed the highlights, we shadow the folds applying shaper touches, helping to better define the volumes of fabric.

Finally to unify and add tones, we are going to apply an intermediate tone with a mixture of color glazes of the base color with a pinch of green, to disguise the transitions between each of the layers.

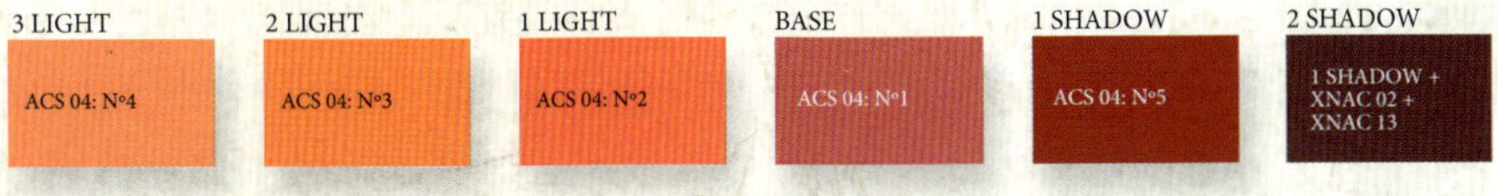

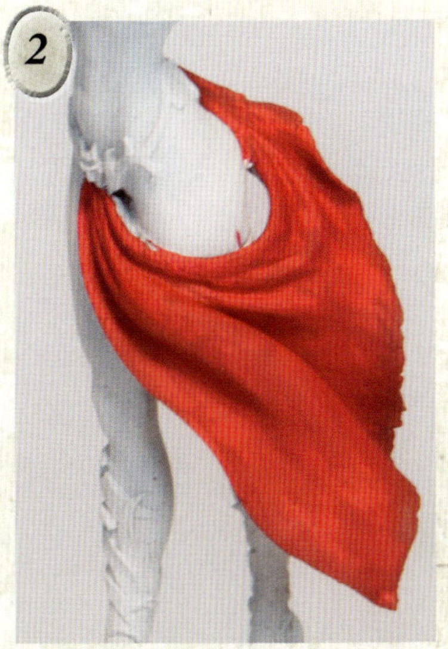

1. Primer.
2. Base.
3. First highlight.
4. Second highlight.

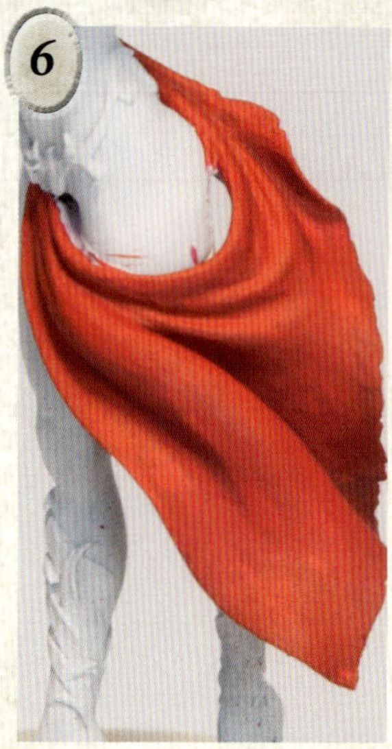

5. First shadow.
6. Third highlight.
7. Second shadow.
8. Application of glazes to show wear.

Painting fabrics with airbrush and brush

In recent years, the introduction of this tool has changed our way of interpreting and painting miniatures. We cannot mention a certain airbrush painting style because the vast majority of figure painters that have learned airbrush painting have done it on their own, developing their own individual techniques.

We have chosen a figure with, ironically, a lot of life: The undead, Menhom, Dark Shadow (WS-10)

We shall start by applying a base color. We used a green color and then we dilute it with the Athinner-01 and apply it evenly to all the nooks and crannies.

We highlight the figure by spraying with the airbrush from above, in the same way that a light bulb would affect the piece. In this case, we chose an overhead lighting.

To apply the second highlight, you shall use a lighter tone and focus on the points where light is more intense. In this way we show greater contrast between the lighter top surfaces and the lower ones, thereby reinforcing the feeling of the zenithal light that is affecting the piece.

We operate in a very similar way for the shadows. We darken the shadows by adding some black to the color used for the base. However, this time we turn the figure completely upside down and darken the opposite part of the illuminated folds.

For the second shadow, we enhance the green color of the fabric by adding a little red to the first shadow mixture. As they are complementary colors, this will highlight the green more giving the whole a greater chromatic richness.

The next step is to sharpen terminations or cuts in the fabric, to limit and define them, with a lighter tone similar to the second highlight.

Finally, we want to give a dirty and natural look to the bottom of the fabric, we cannot forget that he is not dead and that he is dragging himself on the ground, this will add realism to the miniature. To do this, simply apply a diluted drizzle of brown tones over the lower part of the fabric that will be strengthened when we put the figure on his terrain.

2

3

4

5

6

7

8

9

1. *Primer.*

2. *Base coat.*

3. *How to apply a light with an airbrush.*

4. *First light.*

5. *Second light.*

6. *How to apply a shadow with an airbrush.*

7. *First shadow.*

8-9. *Second shadow and tone.*

10

11

12

2 LIGHT	1 LIGHT	BASE	1 SHADOW	2 SHADOW	SPECIAL
XNAC 13	XNAC 06 + XNAC 43	XNAC 06	XNAC 06 + XNAC 30	XNAC 06 + XNAC 02 + XNAC 30	DUST XNAC 52

10. *Outlining.*

11-12. *Outlining and weathering.*

Another example of fabric with airbrush and paintbrush

Menhom, Dark Shadow
WS-10

Painting leather

by Diego Esteban

In this section we will learn how to paint different types of leather using different parts of the same figure: Urmuth, Scars of War (WS-15) A piece of leather that he wears as a skirt and the straps at the top.

The most important thing to bear in mind when painting a certain type of leather is to choose carefully the base color. The choice of this color will depend on the colors of other elements of the figure, and it will also influence the behavior of the highlights and shadows. When painting leather we have to think of the characteristics that make us differentiate it from other materials. One of them is the fact that newly tanned leather has a fully satin finish, while when it is worn it tends to stay matte. If we create these finishing effects for different parts of a piece or type of leather, we will have managed to imitate the material perfectly.

Textured leather

When painting this type of leather, applying the base color plays a central role, as we can see in the image below. Highlights and shadows are next and it is very important to know how to apply them to accomplish some of the effects. We cannot forget the intermediate tones, especially in the areas of shadows where we use the base color and complementary colors to achieve a greater chromatic quality.

We prime the leather in a light color: white or grey. We must always bear in mind that the color of the primer will impact the finishing of the piece. The light base will help us accentuate the tones that we will use.

We apply them with a brush and in a heterogeneous way over the base color, which will create a light texture. We shall use a deep brown.

A sponge will help us to lighten and get a natural texture, reinforcing the existing base. We must focus on the upper part of the leather and those worn and torn parts by applying a mixture of the leather base color and the flesh color, in order to get the lighter tone needed for both the highlighting and the weathering.

We will apply a diluted wash of brown ink (without removing the excess of water from the brush) to shade the areas opposite the light on those less worm ones. We should also apply a second highlight with the brush to enhance the heavy leather texture.

Now mix a little bit of brown ink with green ink and apply a second wash, adding a different tone to this second shadow.

It's time to outline. Firstly, we use the highlight tone creating a worn effect and accentuating the cuts on the surface. This will reinforce the areas of maximum wear, such as the seams' edges. Later, use black to do the same outlining and defining all the different parts, including the seams.

This is an example of the importance of using different tones of the colors on a piece. Now, instead of using green as we did in the second shadow, we will use red. As you can see, it simply changes its appearance by slightly changing one color.

1

3 LIGHT	2 LIGHT	1 LIGHT	BASE	1 SHADOW	2 SHADOW	MIDTONE	SPECIAL
XNAC 42	XNAC 43 + XNAC 45	XNAC 49 + XNAC 43	XNAC 49	ACS 06: BROWN INK	ACS 06: BROWN INK + GREEN INK	ACS 06: GREEN INK	ACS 06: BROWN INK + RED INK

1. *Primer.*

2. *Base color.*

3. *How you texture using a sponge.*

4. *Textured by a sponge.*

5. *How to do an ink wash.*

6. *Ink wash.*

7. *Parts definition and second highlights.*

8. *Second ink wash.*

9. *Highlighting and definition.*

10-11. *Shadow outlining.*

12. *Leather with another tone.*

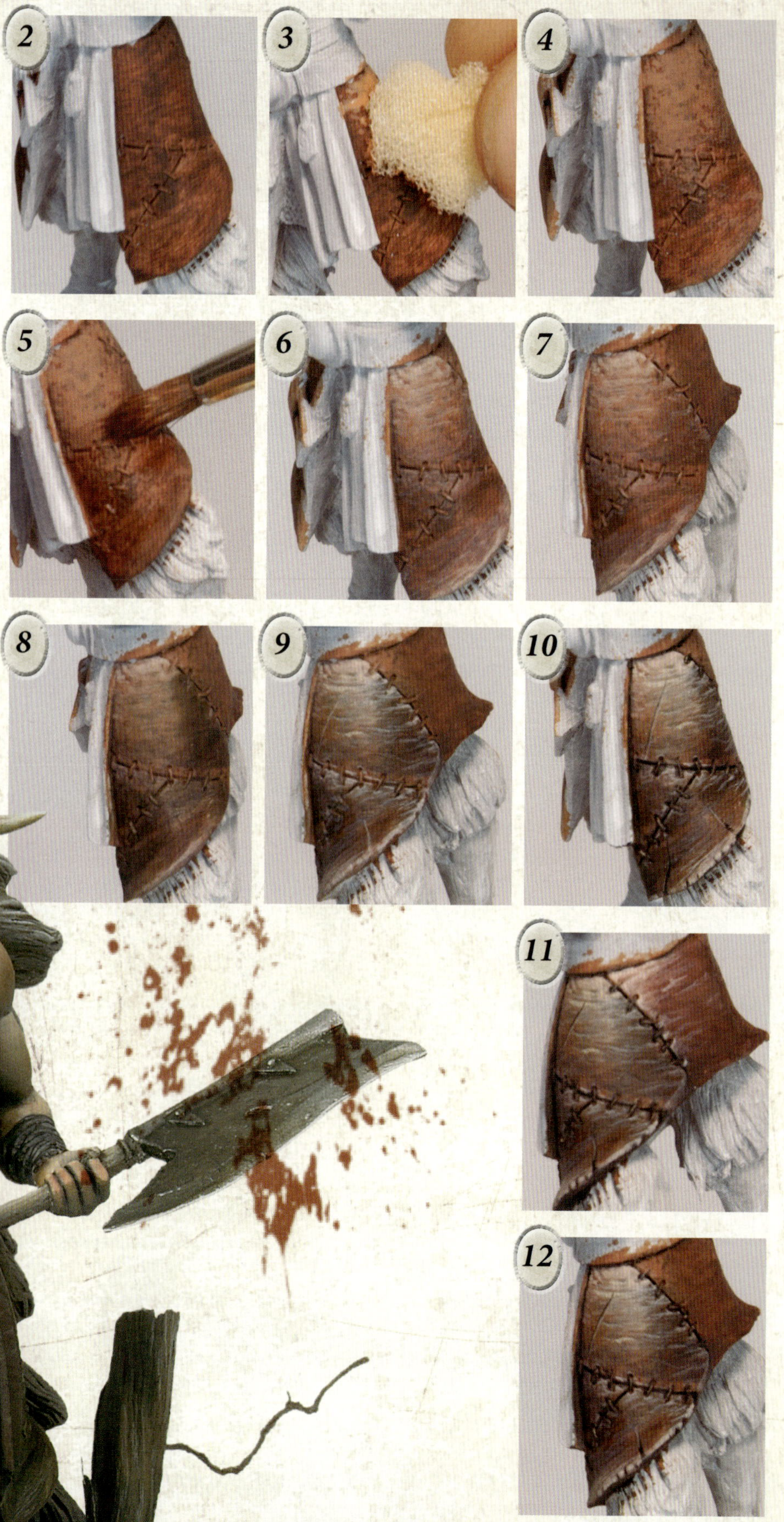

Another example of leather

Urmuth, Scars of War
WS-15

Smooth leather

Let's simulate smooth leather straps with paint. Again we use a light color to Prime.

The smooth leather effect requires applying evenly the base color, unlike the textured leather. We will use a brown tone as a base color.

The lighting is overhead and, therefore, progressive. In this case, we have used a beige color to start the first highlights with a brush. As you can see, we used this same color to enhance the edges of the straps.

A peculiarity of the smooth leather is that the less worn areas tend to be of a satin finish. The effect is easy to replicate by the use of brown glazes with black ink for shading.

We return to illuminate the top of the belt, making small cuts on the edges to create the worn effect in the areas of friction.

At the end we apply the second shadow with a mixture of black and brown ink, reinforcing the satin effect of leather on that area, while we define the piece by outlining the edges creating the maximum worn effect with beige, and leaving those parts in a matte finish.

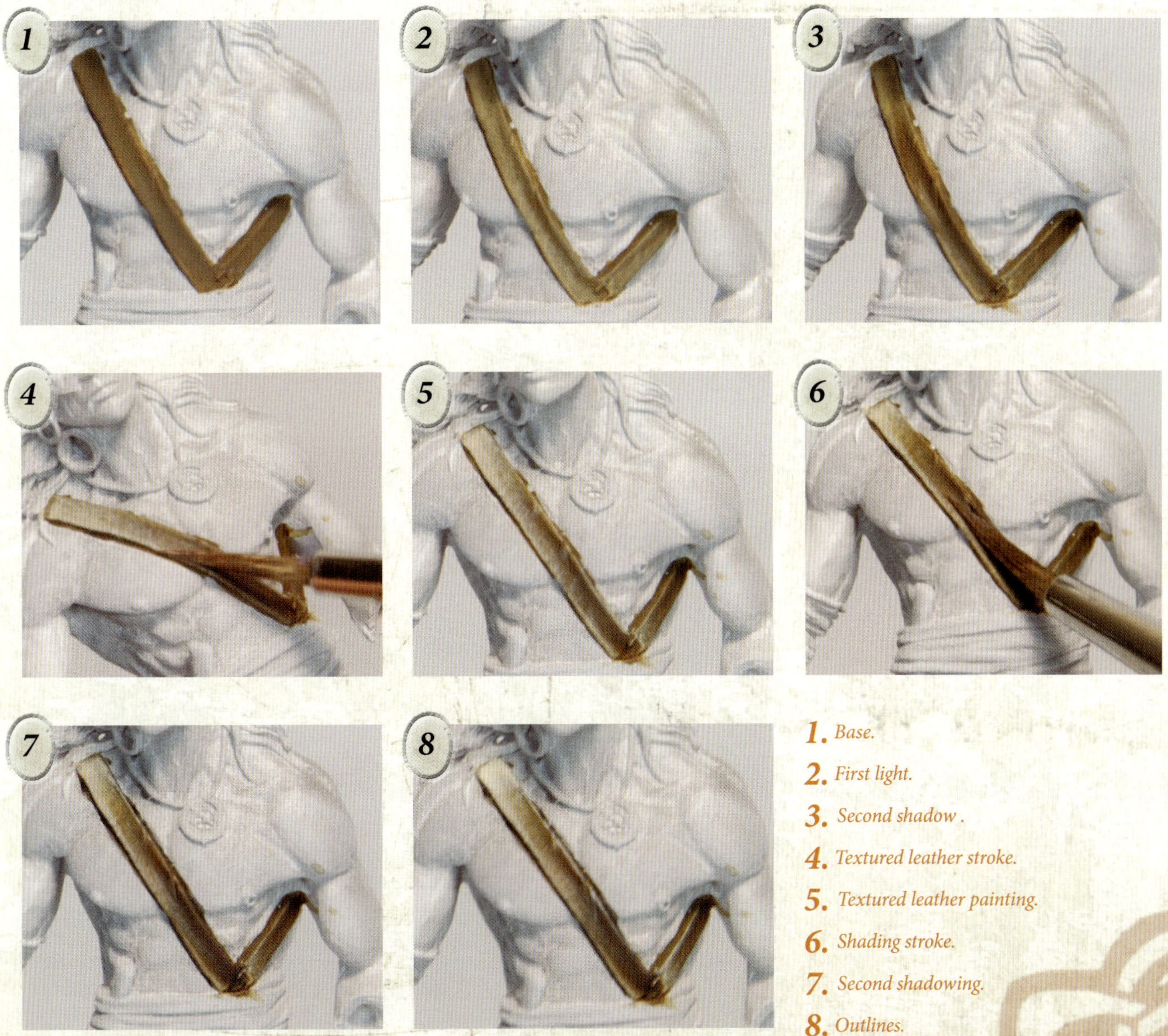

1. Base.
2. First light.
3. Second shadow .
4. Textured leather stroke.
5. Textured leather painting.
6. Shading stroke.
7. Second shadowing.
8. Outlines.

3 LIGHT	2 LIGHT	1 LIGHT	BASE	1 SHADOW	2 SHADOW
XNAC 42	XNAC 41	XNAC 05 + XNAC 41	XNAC 05	ACS 06: ROWN INK + YELLOW INK	ACS 06: BROWN INK + BLACK INK

8

Freehand

by Diego Esteban

Freehand painting is commonly used for fabric decorations, shields, banners, and skin (tattoos). It is a very good way to enhance and add details to a figure. It is important to consider the surface highlights on which it is being drawn and also the drawing itself. The tiny details require a good accuracy and a brush in perfect condition.

During this process, we will finish the cape of Zwëothel (WS-31).

The first step for creating our freehand painting is to design it on a piece of paper. It is very important to choose the motif that we want to paint to make sure it fits in the surface where it is going be located. On the other hand, the design should have a certain relationship with the subject of the figure.

We draw our design on the fabric with a brush. In order to do this, we use a mixture of diluted black and Navy Blue colors, since we want our drawing to be black and also to have a little bit of the color of the fabric, in case we need to correct any mistake.

Now, we need to fill in the freehand drawing with the base color. We use the same colors that we have already used for the sketch but this time excluding the color of the fabric, and less diluted.

For the highlighting, we follow the same process as with the fabric. We need to apply the highlights with a brush focusing on the areas of light at the top of the folds, mixing the base color of the freehand drawing with some ochre.

During the shading process, we need to darken the opposite parts simulating the shadows of the folds.

We finish the process by defining and shaping the more illuminated parts of the fabric. For this, we use the same color we used previously for the second fabric highlights in order to finish the drawing.

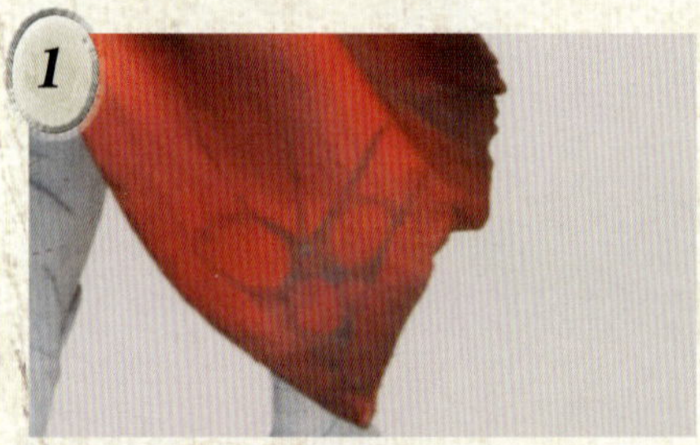

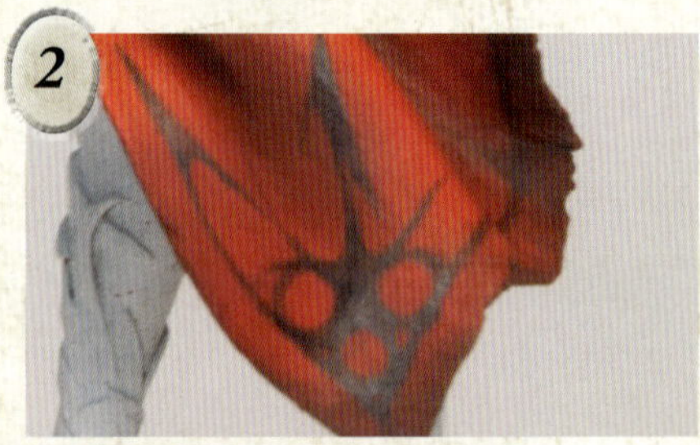

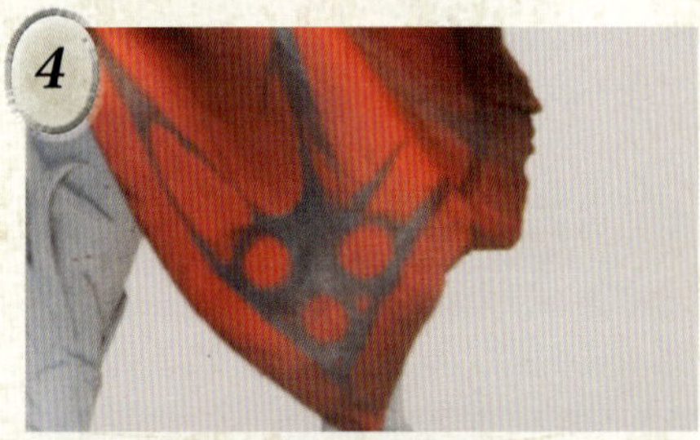

1. *Drawing outline.*
2. *Drawing fill.*
3. *Drawing lightning.*
4. *Highlights.*
5. *Shadowing.*
6. *Definition.*
7. *Completed Freehand painting.*

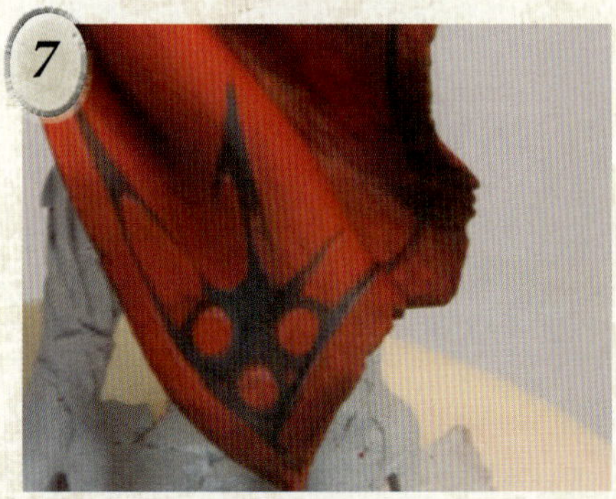

1 LIGHT	BASE	1 SHADOW
XNAC 11 + XNAC 42	XNAC 11 + XNAC 02	XNAC 02

Tattoos

The fantasy world is full of symbolism, whether it is magical, or decorative. Tattoos are important on such figures. Sometimes they are superficial (ritual paintings). One way or another they are often used as elements requiring great harmony between the skin and the drawing. Now we will learn how to produce them.

Once we have the skin on which we want to work finished, we chose the "tattoo" motif and execute the tattoo design on paper.

We sketch the drawing onto the skin of Brogan with a mixture of Navy Blue and the base of very dilute skin color. When we are sure that the design is correct, and in the right area, we fill in with Navy Blue mixed with the color we used for the shade of skin. It will help to create the effect of a rather old tattoo...

The lighting of the figure falls mainly by the upper part of the shoulder. It should take into account the natural lighting of the skin and the volume over which we are drawing the tattoo. Added to the base color, is a little light skin color.

Shading of the skin tone will also guide where the shadows go on the tattoo. As you can see, we use a black color on the bottom.

It is important to use a glaze over the tattoo with a color based on the skin. The feeling we get is depth, finding it under the skin... Thusly toning the skin tattoo with the color of both.

If we want our tattoo to appear to be freshly applied, what we should do is to sharpen the edge of the drawing with the color of the skin to outline it as much as possible and leave it perfect, in this case Brogan has had his tattoo for quite a while.

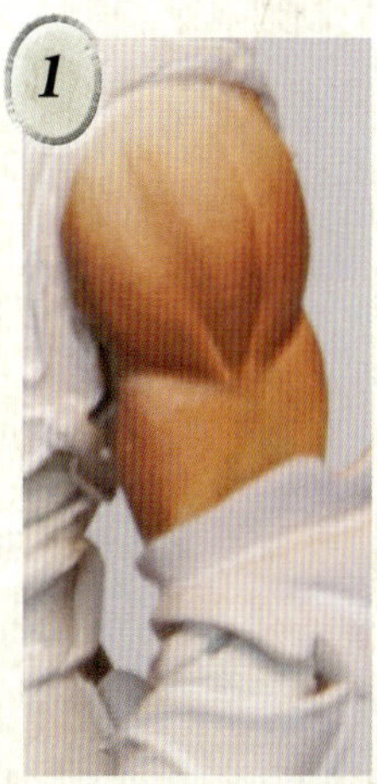

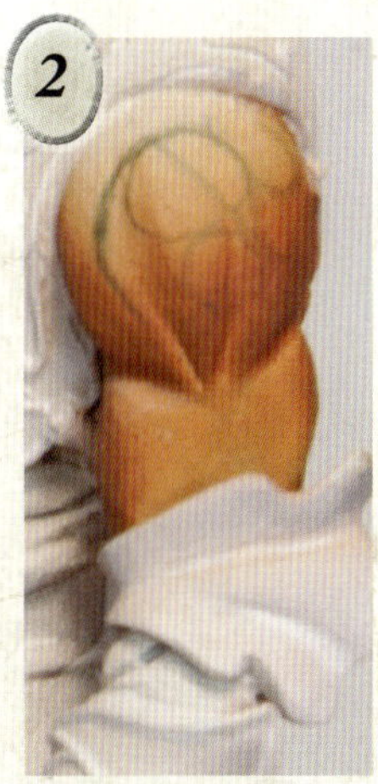

1. Base color of the arm painted.
2. Outline of the drawing.
3. Filling in the drawing.
4. Highlighting of the drawing.
5. Shadowing with a brush.
6. Shadowed.
7. Glazes for unification with the skin.
8. Finished tattoo.

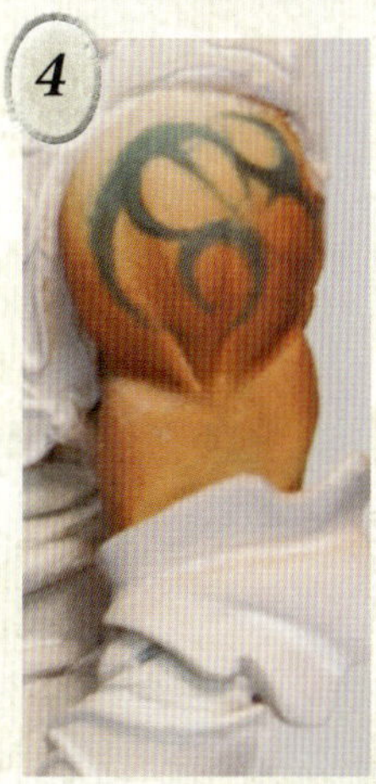

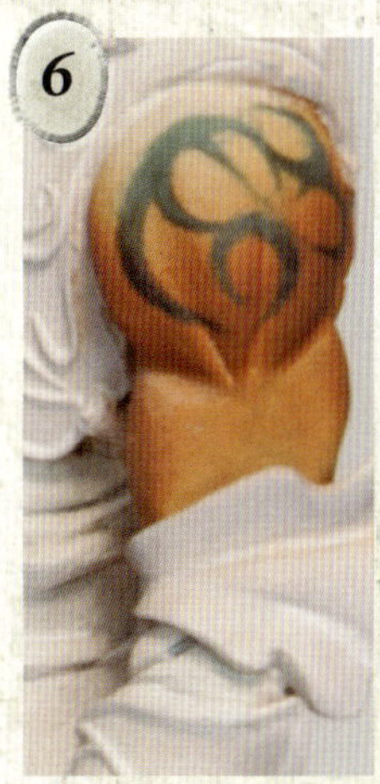

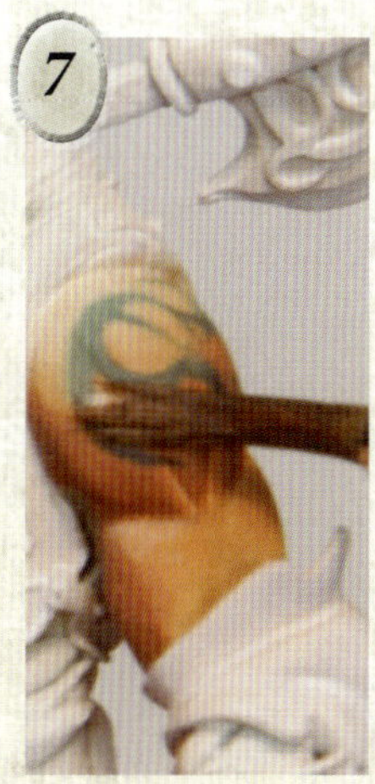

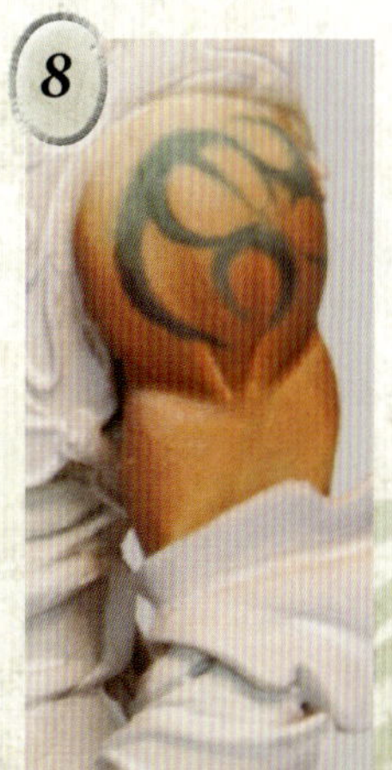

2 LIGHT	1 LIGHT	BASE	1 SHADOW	SPECIAL
XNAC 11 + ACS 01: Nº3	XNAC 11 + ACS 01: Nº5	XNAC 11	XNAC 03	ACS 01: Nº1

Painting gems

by Diego Esteban

Painting gems is easy if we take into account how light behaves when going through the mineral. Gemstones refract light and send it out the side opposite form which it enters, so we have to be able to copy this effect. It requires a very clean technique, because otherwise it may seem opaque and without volume. It is important to remember that gems are usually polished and, if we do not establish a good gradient, we will lose this feeling. We will consider two different ways of working depending on whether we want to paint a light or a dark gem.

Translucent gem

In the first case, we apply a deep green color as the base color.

If we imagine that the light enters through the top right of the gem, let's start by shading this area using a mixture of color glazes of a blacker base color, or even black directly.

As we have seen above, light is reflected on the opposite side from where it enters, and, therefore, we are going to bring light to the lower left with a brighter green than the one used for the base color.

At this point, we still see the gem incomplete. We need to apply a lighter shade on the most illuminated area and a touch of extreme light intensity in the shaded area, to simulate a real gem.

We apply yellow ink glazes to smooth it and thus to give it the luminosity of carved gems, like the one we are painting.

Finally, we should apply strong highlights using white on the darkest part and which affects the light in the stone.

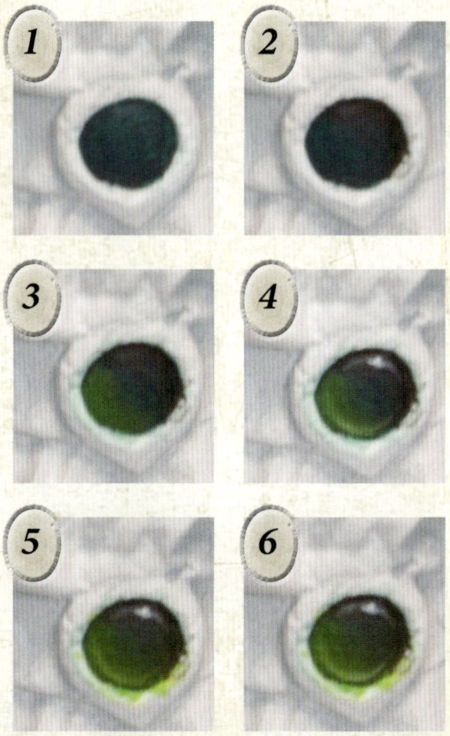

1. *Base coat.*
2. *First shadow.*
3. *First highlight.*
4. *Points of light.*
5. *Yellow ink wash.*
6. *Second ink wash and outlining.*

Ithandïr,
Blade of Eternity
WS-01

2 LIGHT	1 LIGHT	BASE	1 SHADOW	MIDTONE
XNAC 01	XNAC 13	XNAC 14	XNAC 02	ACS 06 : YELLOW INK

Polished gem

In this other example, we will learn how to paint a darker stone, making another interpretation of the behavior of light, in this case the opposite one.

As in the previous process, we start with the base color, in this case, a very dark turquoise.

The type of stone that we are going to paint is not as transparent as the gem. It is more like a polished stone, which also shows some very intense reflections. Now the light does not go through the stone, but instead is reflected in it behaving similarly to other opaque material. Therefore, if the stone is receiving the light from above, this will be the area that we will paint with a greater intensity of light, and we will use more shadows for the bottom.

Once we have finished the painting process, we apply a thin layer of satin varnish.

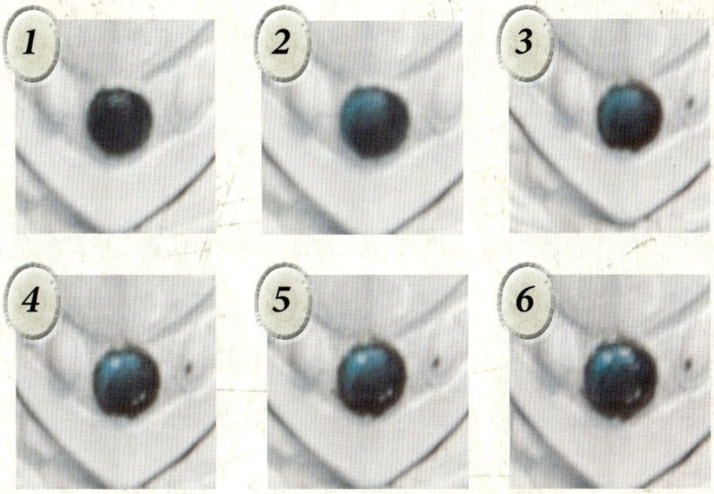

1. *Base coat.*
2. *First highlight.*
3. *First shadow.*
4. *Points of light.*
5. *External outlining.*
6. *Varnish.*

2 LIGHT	1 LIGHT	BASE	1 SHADOW	MIDTONE
XNAC 01	XNAC 15	XNAC 11	XNAC 02	XNAC 59 SATIN VARNISH

Other examples of different colors of gems

Khaerus, the Summoner
WS-04

Falkar, Wandering Sword
ws-19

Non-metallic metal

by Diego Esteban

Fantasy figures usually have several metal parts, such as armor, weapons, shields etc. There are two different ways of painting metals. For the first one we would use metallic pigment colors and for the second we would use non-metallic colors. The NMM painting is a technique that has been used for fine art during centuries. The biggest problem you can encounter when applying this technique to miniature figure painting is that you have to create this effect on a three-dimensional surface, and this is not easy. In order to work in this effect, you must take into account three basic guidelines: brightness, reflections and the sharp contrasts between the highlights and the shadows.

There are endless possible mixtures of colors that we can create for this effect. This is why there are specific colors sets in the market for inexperienced painters that provide already done mixtures to carry out this process and obtain a very satisfactory result.

Painting non-metallic metal with airbrush and paintbrush

Now we are going to learn how to paint a sword with an airbrush using the non-metallic colors of the Andrea Color Paint Set ACS-12.

Apply the base color evenly over the entire surface, and then illuminate it with the first light of the set. However, we will not do it in the usual area of highlighting, but we will begin to simulate the reflection that would have the metallic pigment if we had used that to paint the sword as you can see on the picture.

We enhance this light effect by adding a second layer of highlight focusing on simulating the reflections of the metal.

Now we begin to see some metallic appearance on the sword. We are going to darken the sword using the first shadow from the non-metallic metals paint set, always trying to picture how the material's shadow would really look. For the shadows, follow the same procedure we have previously used for the highlights.

We can see here how we apply this first shadow by spraying the airbrush from the bottom and broadly in the areas that still maintain the base color.

Sharpening the edges of the weapon with the second highlight from the set will help us find out if we are on track. This sharp contrast will give us a non-metallic effect pattern. We will also add a maximum highlight point with pure white to simulate metal reflections.

For the same reason that the material reflects the light to the maximum in white, the maximum shadow is black. We create a smooth gradient with the airbrush from intense light to intense dark.

Some of the outlining we applied before to check if the effect was working is lost when we add maximum shadows with the airbrush. Therefore, we have to go back and sharpen all the corners and edges of the sword.

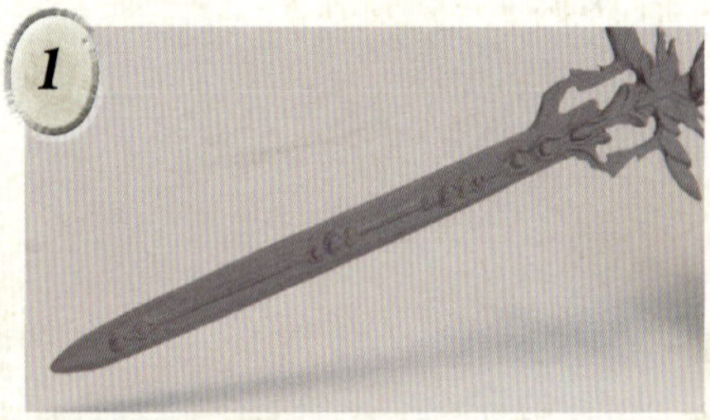

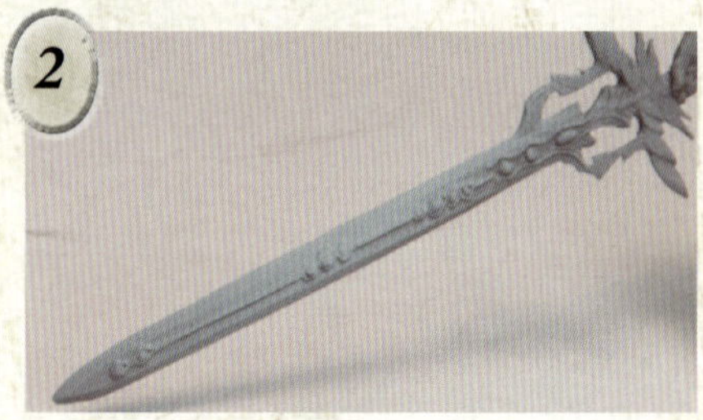

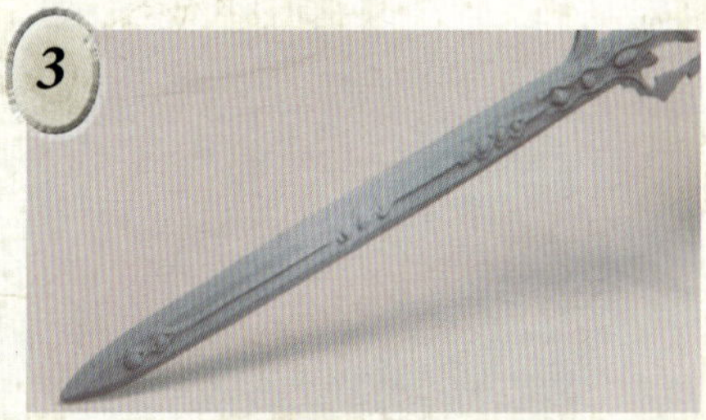

3 LIGHT	2 LIGHT	1 LIGHT	BASE	1 SHADOW	2 SHADOW
ACS 12: Nº4	ACS 12: Nº3	ACS 12: Nº 2	ACS 12: Nº1	ACS 12: Nº5	ACS 12: Nº6

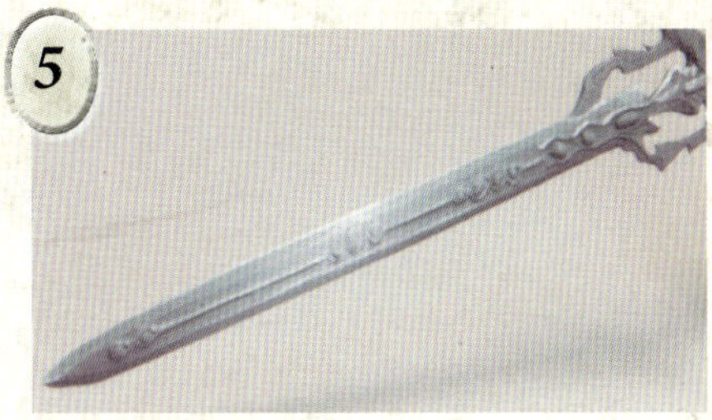

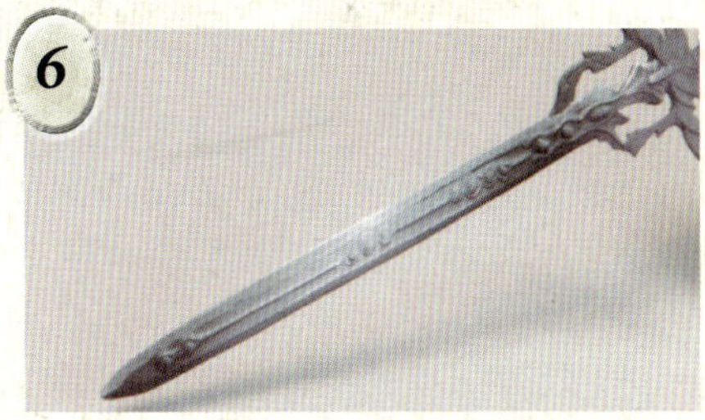

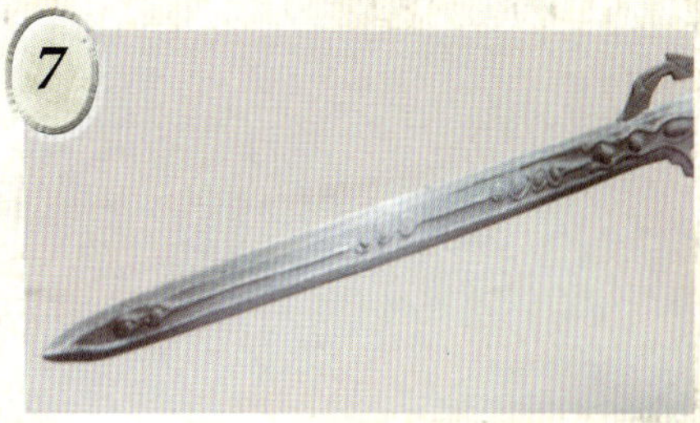

1. Base.

2. First highlight.

3. Second highlight.

4. First shadow.

5. Brush outline.

6. Second shadow.

7. Outline and definition.

Painting non-metallic metal with paintbrush

If you do not have an airbrush or you do not want use it, you can also do it with a brush. Make sure that the transitions from one color to another are as little visible as possible. Harsh changes will make it lose the metal effect. In order to show you the brush painting process we have used some of the colors included in the non-metallic Andrea Color Paint Set as a base combining them with other colors from that same range, to create a non-metallic effect with a different look.

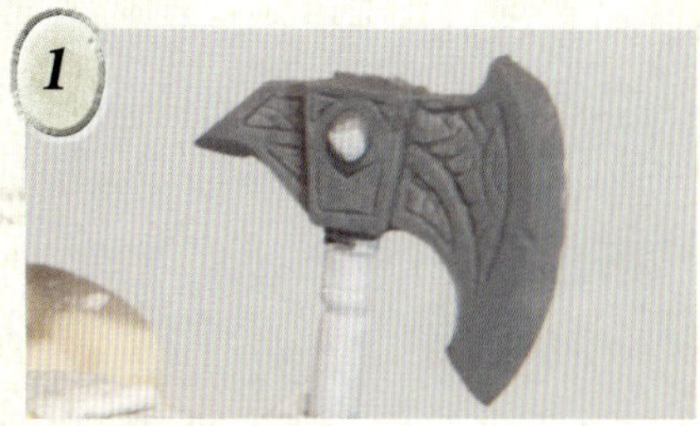

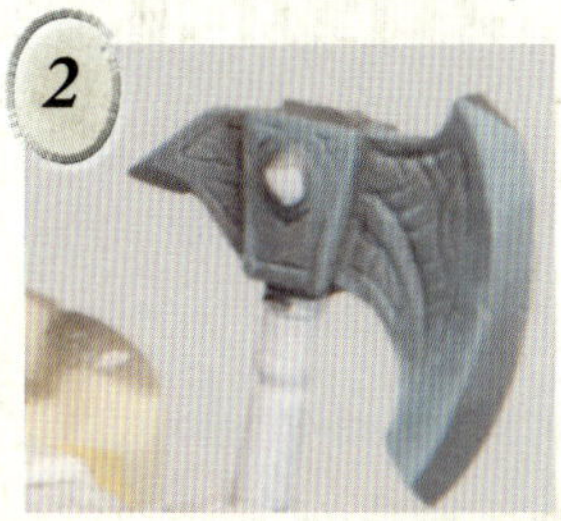

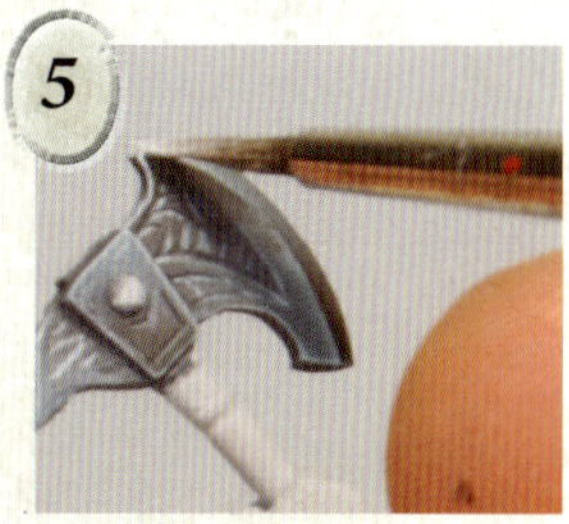

1. Base.

2. First light.

3. First shadow.

4. Second light.

5. Brush outline .

6. Outlining with highlights.

7. Outlining with shadows.

8. Second shadow and shades.

9. Reflection stripped effect.

3 LIGHT	2 LIGHT	1 LIGHT	BASE	1 SHADOW	2 SHADOW	MIDTONE	SPECIAL
2 LIGHT + XNAC 01	ACS 12: Nº3	ACS 12: Nº2	ACS 12: Nº1	ACS 12: Nº5 + XNAC 08	XNAC 03	XNAC 03 + XNAC 52	XNAC 30

Painting metal and rust

by Diego Esteban

Today we can find many acrylic paints with metallic pigments, which are conceived and designed to paint miniatures. Apparently they all look the same, but when it comes to painting, we can find differences. A pigment is used, for example, to keep a certain degree of clumping from happening allowing diluted brushwork or giving a base to cover the surface without gumming up the area; so these are some of the aspects that we need to consider. If they can also be used with an airbrush, without causing a jam of paint in the nozzle, we will have the perfect paint for all the possible options.

The inks are very good complements for the metallic paints. They give us the possibility of creating a variety of intermediate tones and deep shadows.

Silver

Let's see how to work with metallic pigments on the shoulder and chest of Dagor Ancient Fury (WS-23).

We apply black primer. The primer color influences the final result of the figures making them lighter or darker depending on the color of the primer.

The black primer will allow us to see if we have covered the figure's details completely and evenly to paint a metal base coat, in this case silver. Later we will begin another process for the gold color.

We use the Andrea Color Silver Paint Set (ACS-07). We apply the base color in the same way we have previously explained, and then we will illuminate the base coat with the first light of the set. This first light layer will affect the metal finishing.

Having already illuminated the piece, we will add a light wash of black paint mixed with a very diluted brown ink over the entire piece. This layer will get into all the nooks and crannies, creating the first shadow. Although it is a little bit blurry, we will begin to see the shapes and filigree from the carved metal.

After this wash, we have lost part of the highlighting that we previously gave to the metal, so we will have to add it back.

We apply a second coat of the same wash we used above reinforcing the shadow that was created in different parts, in this case, the shoulder pad.

Again, the wash blurs the details so we need to redefine them with the base color from the set. Now the metal has that brown tone that creates the corrosion effect. We must not forget that the figure is an old monkey man who lived a thousand adventures in this armor. Therefore, it has become worn and rusty over the years.

Now we need to strengthen the oxide, which naturally has been accumulating itself at the bottom of each of the recesses. In this case, the rust will be orange-brown. We use a dark orange tone that then will need to be highlighted to define it.

It is very important to know the color that should be used to oxidize a piece of metal. If we use an inappropriate color we will not get the feeling of rust that we want. The best thing to do is to look for information on the material you want to create in order to achieve the desired effect.

1

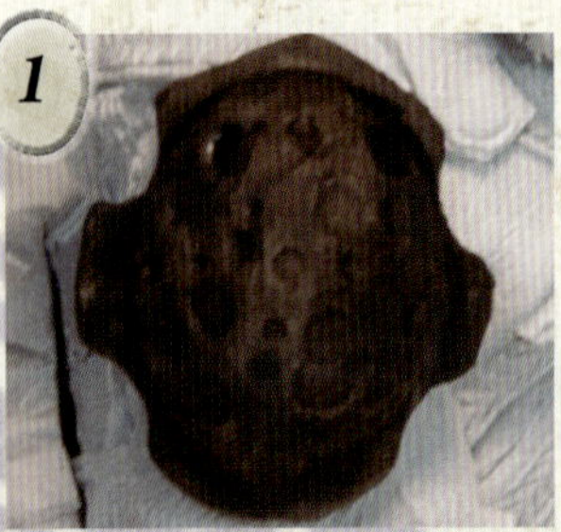

2

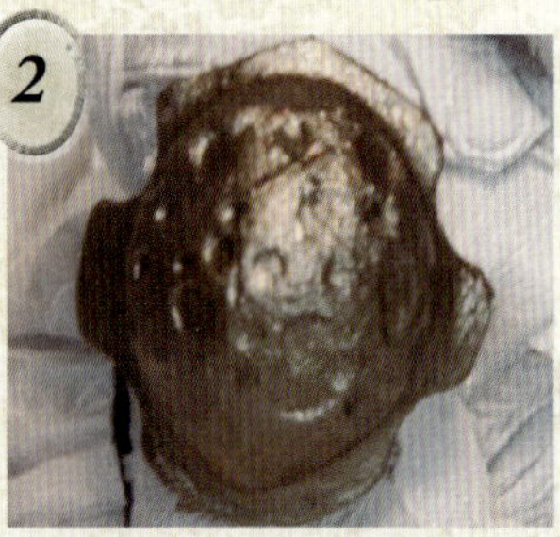

3

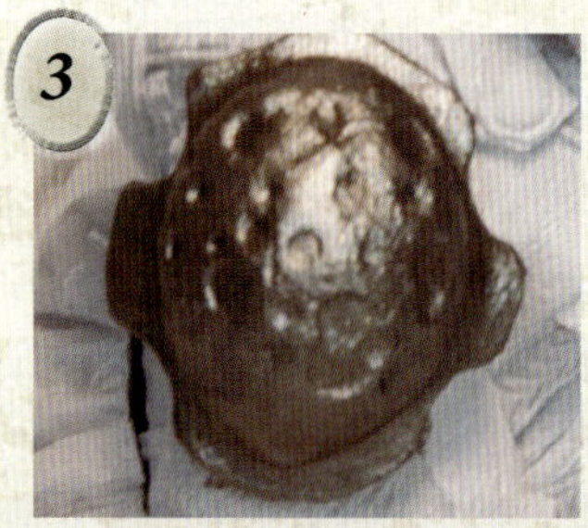

4

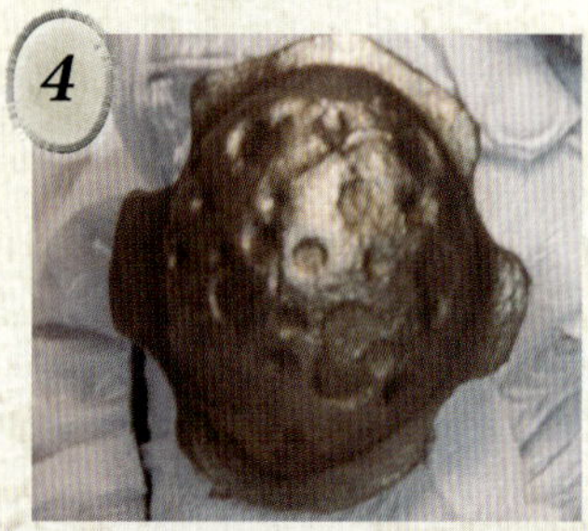

2 LIGHT	1 LIGHT	BASE	1 SHADOW	2 SHADOW	SPECIAL
ACS 07: Nº2	ACS 07: Nº1	ACS 07: Nº3	XNAC 02 + ACS 07: BROWN INK	1 SHADOW + XNAC 02 +	OUTLINE ACS 07: Nº2 WASH XNAC 35

1. Primer.
2. Base color.
3. First highlight.
4. Shaded by washing.
5. Second highlight.
6. Shaded and toned with washes.
7. Stronger highlight.
8. Shadowing the oxide.
9. Highlighting the oxide.
10. Outlining and cuts.

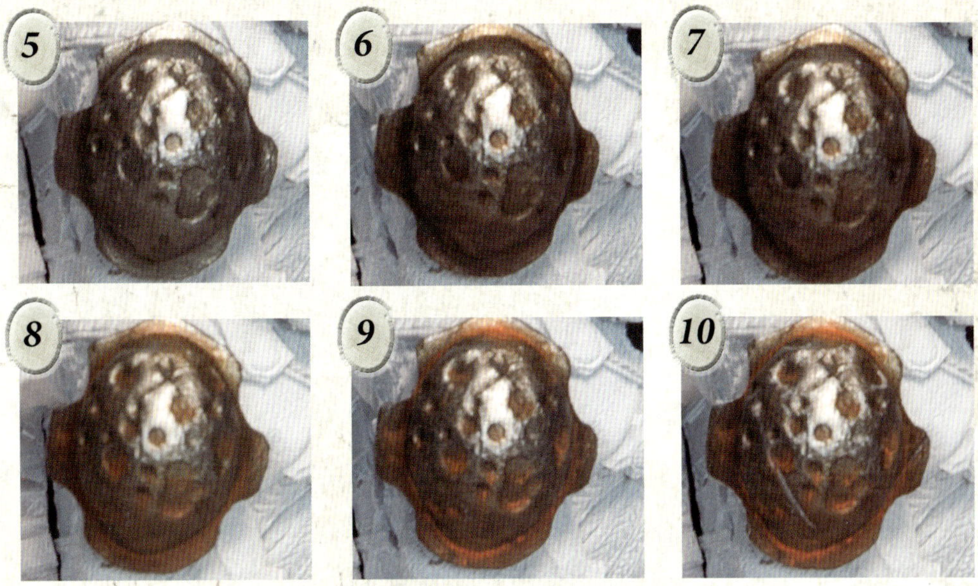

11.2

Gold

We will show now how the process would be if we would like to create gold on one of the plates that this miniature has on its chest. The highlighting and shadowing processes are similar to the ones previously explained, logically varying the tones for each particular case. The different thing about this process will be the turquoise oxide of the gold.

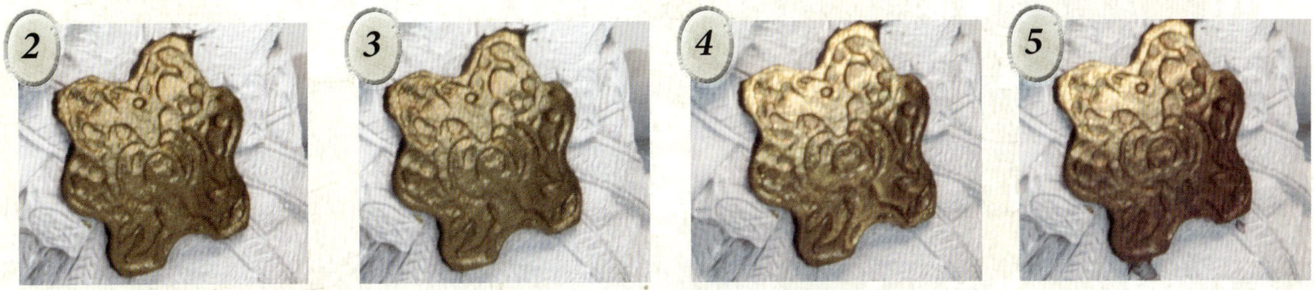

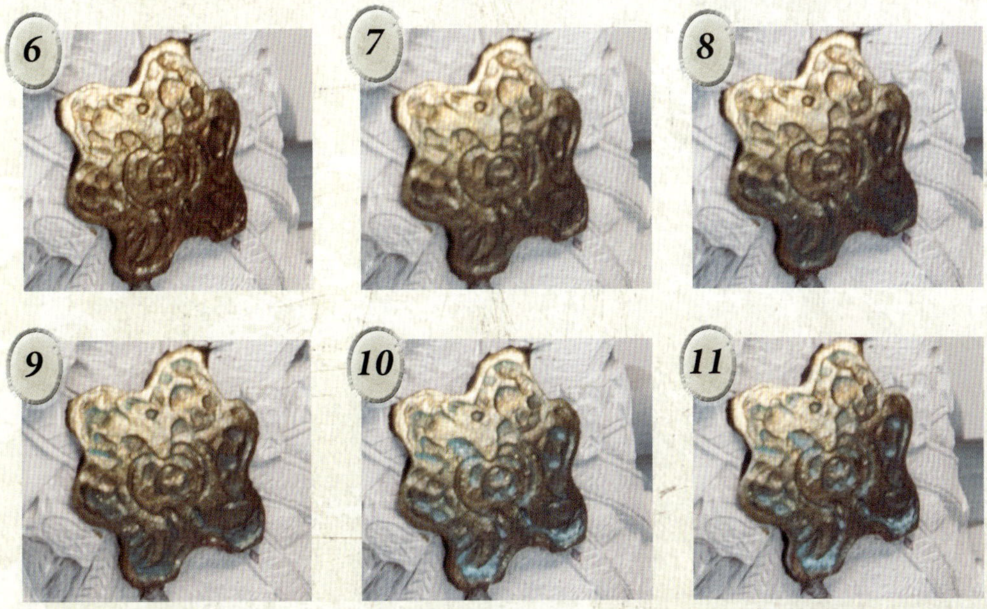

1. Primer.
2. Base coat.
3. First highlight.
4. Second highlight.
5. First shadow.
6. Highlights.
7. Second shadow.
8. Oxide tone.
9. Second oxide tone.
10. Oxide highlights.
11. Light outline.

3 LIGHT	2 LIGHT	1 LIGHT	BASE	1 SHADOW	2 SHADOW	RUST
ACS 08: Nº2	1 LIGHT + ACS 08: Nº2	ACS 08: Nº1	ACS 08: Nº3	XNAC 02 + ACS 08: BLUE INK + HAZEL INK	XNAC 02 + XNAC15	XNAC15 + XNAC 01 / XNAC 15

Painting scenery and terrain

Despite being very important for the presentation of a figure, we usually do not spend too much time in the development of the groundwork. It is a secondary issue and most of the time we leave it until the end of the process. It is really important to know how to choose the main view of the figure. It is generally the view photographed for the box art of the figure. If we do not have that image, it is appropriate to assemble the kit so we can identify which is the best angle for viewing the figure. In this tutorial we will learn how to take advantage of the bases that are included with all miniatures in a fast and easy way.

Simple terrain

by Diego Esteban and Julio Cabos

Specifically, let's create an autumn terrain for Drünegar (WS-03).

In the first place, and to give a greater presence and elegance to our figure, we will look for a base or wooden block in a color, shape and size appropriate for the figure that you want to place on it. Almost all the figures come with a base that we will use now, since our miniature fits perfectly onto this element. To avoid the metal base overlapping the wooden pedestal, grind the surface with a cutter. We apply the cyanocrylate glue to the base and let it dry. This is necessary, since normally the pedestals are coated with varnish which fills its pores and glue cannot adhere well to it.

We use two-component putty to integrate the metal base with the wooden block, thus complementing the rest of the terrain. Once the putty is dry, make a mixture of white glue and water to add sand and small pieces of bark to the base to make stones. Small stones that can be found outside can also be used.

1. *Materials.*

2. *Metal piece bonded to the base.*

3. *Base filled with putty.*

4. *Sand and stones placement.*

1

2

3

4

The next step is to prime the groundwork in a dark color which will make it easier to paint and to create the atmosphere we are looking for. The terrain, like the figure, will be affected by the same light, but to focus attention on the figure, we can play with the colors of the ground leaving the main view to be the part where the figure attaches. We started painting by applying a base color to the soil and rocks and use the dry brush technique to highlight the stones. This technique consists of giving short and quick strokes with a brush from which we have previously removed almost all the paint onto a paper blotter or piece of fabric, speeding up the work.

With the airbrush, we will unify the whole by applying an intermediate color, which will also help us to create new tones on the ground.

1 LIGHT	BASE COLOR	
XNAC 52	XNAC 02	Terrain base

5

6

7

8

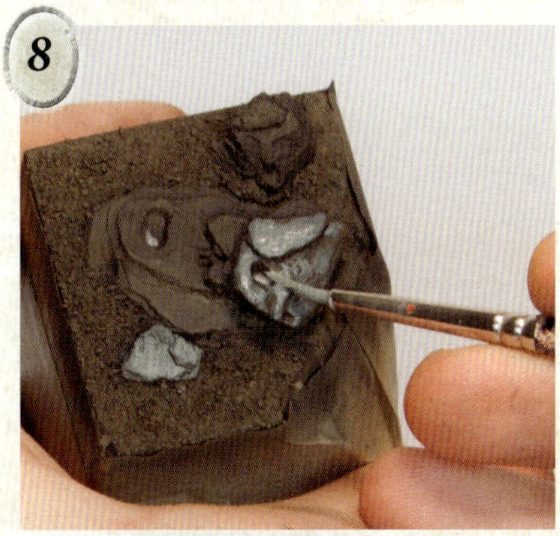

9

10

11

5. Airbrush priming.

6. Base coat.

7. First highlights.

8. How to use the dry brush to paint stones.

9. Dry brush for stones.

10. Airbrush.

11. Dry brush stones.

2 LIGHT	1 LIGHT	BASE COLOR	MIDTONE	
XNAC 02	XNAC 19 + XNAC 04	XNAC 02	XNAC 52	Stones

Add sea foam balls randomly on the ground simulating grass and weeds, an important element to achieve the type of terrain we are trying to simulate. To finally integrate the whole of the groundwork with the figure, we can use some shadow in this case, those employed in painting the leather or fabrics. Thus, the figure and the ground reflect the same atmosphere.

Finally, we attach the figure and add the final details on the ground work to give atmosphere to the autumn season. To do this, add white glue and sprinkle on marjoram leaves. Now it is complete, ready for our showcase!

12. How to take the sea weed.

13. How to use the sea weed.

14. Result of the placement of the seaweed.

We add some majoram leaves on top of a thin coat of a mixture of White glue and water.

Elaborate terrain

by Diego Esteban

We already saw how to prepare simple groundwork for a fantasy figure. Now, we are going to create a more elaborate one, involving several elements. In this case, we are going to represent the scene in which a shaman is dancing around the fire using the figure of Mad Marnik (WS-09).

First, we create a small sketch of the finished scene, to be able to work out the design, making a small study of composition of the scene, so that everything works.

Once we have the idea, then comes the research. Using documentation as a reference for placing the vegetation and other elements in a natural way. Often we find it difficult to capture the idea from our imagination, and that frustrates our attempts to do something more elaborate.

The starting point for the terrain will be to anchor the figure well so it cannot fall. First, add a thick branch following the design and use that branch to support the figure creating a pin that fits perfectly in the hole that we previously drilled in the figure. Now we attach the branch to the pedestal with cyanoacrylate glue, and create the soil with two-component putty, gluing both the metal pin and the branch to the ground. We are adding finer branches to simulate shrubs or trees, in this case, dry ones.

It is time to apply the sand using a mixture of white glue and water. This will accelerate the process of drying of the glue.

1. Materials.

2. Attaching the miniature and trunk with a pin to the pedestal.

3. Covering the base with Putty and setting the pin.

4. Placement of the sand.

2 LIGHT	LIGHT	BASE	MIDTONE	SPECIAL
XNAC 52 + XNAC 43	XNAC 04	XNAC 02	XNAC 52	PIGMENT SET 01

Once we have prepared the groundwork, is time to get down to work, and start to paint it. We'll leave the placement of details and more fragile elements that complicate the painting for later.

Before picking up the brush, we mask off the wooden pedestal so as not to stain it and so that we can use the airbrush without fear, and prime the terrain. We started highlighting the trunk and branches by brush following the pattern of lighting that we used for the shaman.

We use the airbrush to smooth the transition from highlight to shadow. Then we paint the stones with the technique of dry brushing that we explained above. We have to return to work on this area of the ground to add the items that were left off for painting. What we see here are those that we will use to complete the terrain.

5. Primer.

6. Application of dry brush to trunk.

7. First highlight of the trunk.

8. First shadow.

9. Highlighting the sand.

10. Application of dry brush to sand.

11. Highlighting and pigments for the sand.

2 LIGHT	1 LIGHT	BASE	1 SHADOW
XNAC 52 + XNAC 43 + XNAC 13	XNAC 08 + XNAC 52	XNAC 02	XNAC 11 + XNAC 02 + XNAC 29

Attach ball of sea foam to simulate dry grass, weeds, etc. In our composition, you cannot skip the fire, since we are representing a shaman dancing around it. By looking at our documentation that we are researched at the beginning, we paint in the reflections that would be created by a small fire on all the elements of the terrain.

Finally, we only need to mount the figure and the stake on our terrain.

12

13

14

15

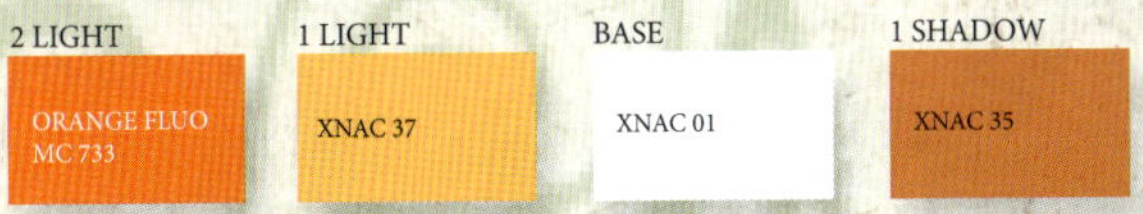

12. Materials for thin vegetation.

13. How the vegetation is placed.

14. Reflections of the bonfire.

15. Glare highlighting.

16. Terrain finished but missing the figure and retouching for unification.

16

Final views.

Other examples of elaborate terrain

Mixed techniques, painting a dragon

by Julio Cabos

Here we are in the last chapter where we will paint a spectacular piece. Now we will be able to put in practice all the techniques that we have learned in this book.

Because of its size and complexity, it is very important to make a preliminary study of the parts that we are going to glue together before we begin to paint, and those which will be attached after being painted. Painting a kit with these features requires patience and, above all, keep a global vision of the whole and do not treat each element independently which can generate in a myriad of colors without an aesthetic sense. We need to prepare a color chart on a sheet of paper, with the main colors of the body and wings that we will use on the dragon. Departing from this idea, we need to think about the lighting and the environment (winter, fire, night, etc.) and also in all the details for the assembly of the kit.

One of the great advantages about working on fantasy figures is that we can let our imagination run free and we do not need to consider the strict historic guidelines or uniformologies. Playing with the effects of light reflection, painting strange metals or almost inhuman faces, are some of the many options that we can choose.

1

2

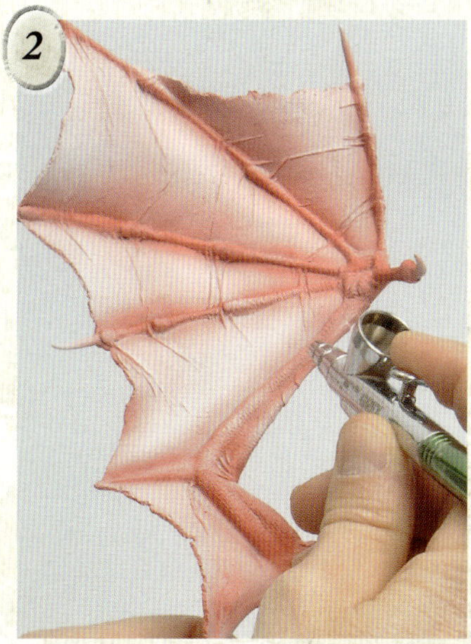

3

4

1. *Apply white primer with an airbrush and start painting the body in a reddish tone on the top and yellow in the bottom. Given the different textures of the body, these first single colors are more of a sketch of the overall tone, than a base color.*

2-3. *Do the same with the wings, although the texture allows us to give it a more detailed finish than in the body.*

4. *We apply the same shade of yellow ochre on the underside of the wings.*

1 LIGHT	BASE	SHADOW	MID TONE	
XNAC 05 + XNAC 40	XNAC 47 + XNAC 35 + ACS 04: Nº1	XNAC 30	ACS 04: Nº4	Airbrush

5. *Return to using the airbrush, with intermediate tone, highlighting the volumes and textures of the body.*

6. *Do the same on the wings.*

7-8. *Apply a shadow to reinforce the skin wrinkles and further darken the plates where they exit the body horns.*

9. *Hereafter, the brush will be our only tool to address the fine detail of the different parts of the dragon.*

10. *The application of glazes with different shades of red, orange and yellow ocher over the different parts of the body, will be that each one of them will have a division, but without losing a sense of the whole.*

11. *Paint the eye of the dragon with Golden Brown XNAC-37.*

12. *Apply a glaze with Golden Yellow ink to highlight the eye's inner contour.*

13. *We get a light to the interior of the eye with a mixture of Yellow and White.*

14. *Several glazes around the eye, starting with a tint of French Orange XNAC-35, working up to Light Yellow XNAC-40, to create an effect of light projected from the inside of the eye.*

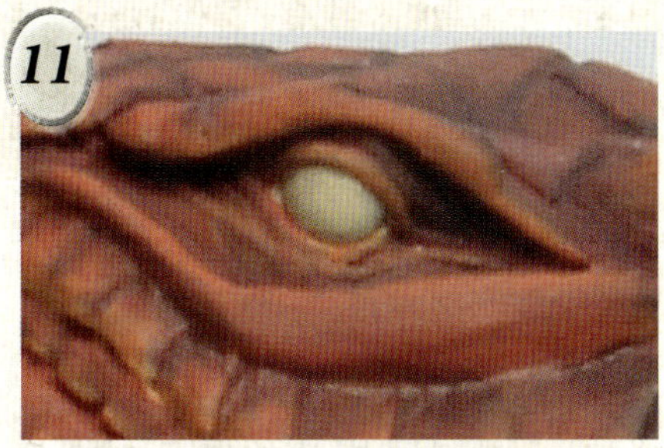

11

12

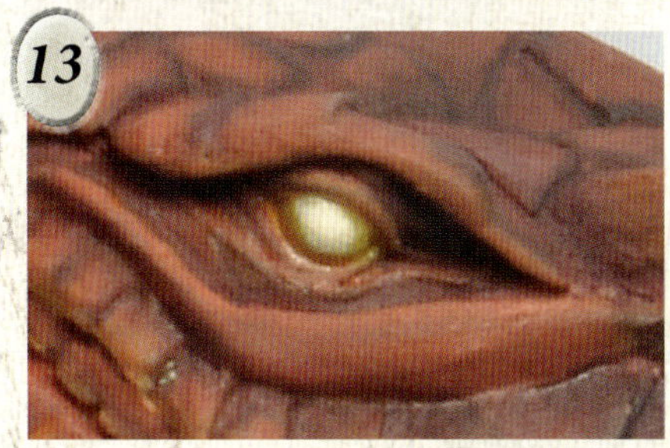

13

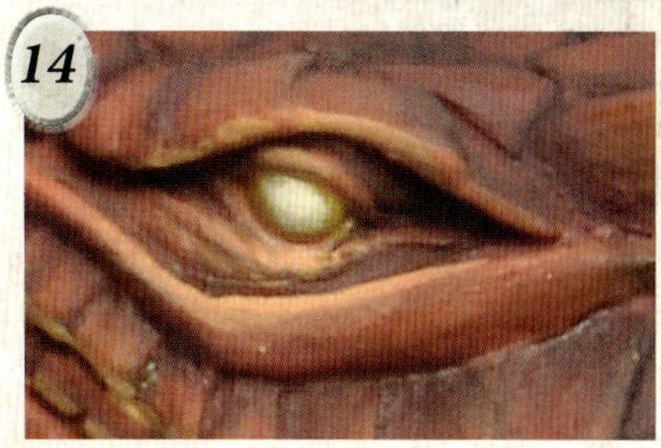

14

15-16. *Following the same guidelines we paint the inside of the mouth, combining the glazes in shades of red and oranges to highlight the deep areas of wrinkles and textures. For most areas, the mixtures should not be so liquid, enabling outlining and accentuating the most prominent wrinkles.*

17. *Detail of the tongue painted, following the same tonal gradation as the rest of the mouth.*

18. *The bit should be painted beforehand and located unglued, between the teeth and the tongue.*

19. *After attaching the top of the head, you can make some adjustments of light and shadows on the treated elements.*

15

16

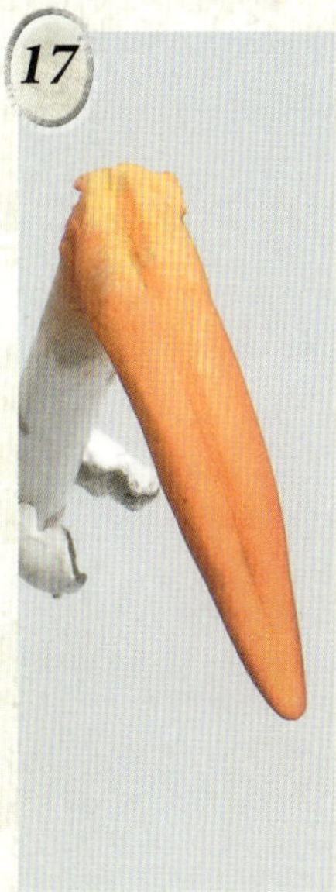

17

18

19

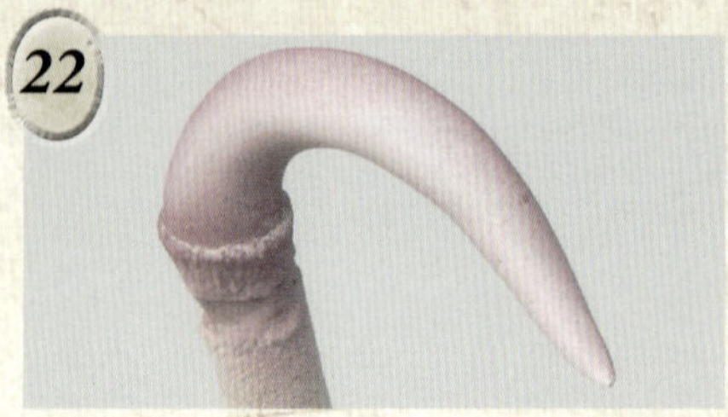

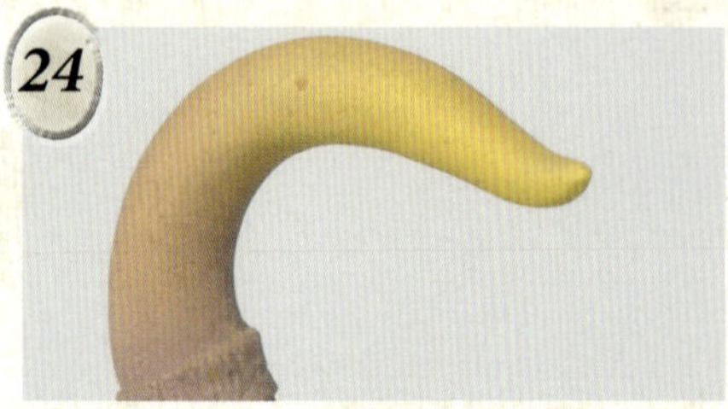

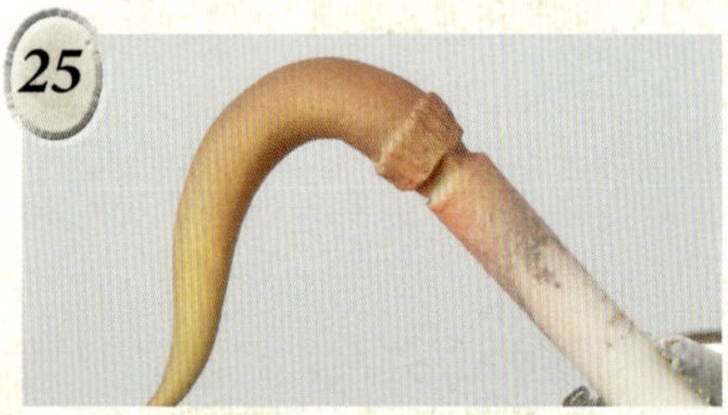

20. *Details of the skin and the right side scales. The tone has become darker and slightly cold, the opposite of the other side which is more illuminated.*

21. *The glazes are mostly the main tools we use in all the processes, due to the countless textures that we can find in the dragon.*

22. *Base color of the horns on the head. We use the airbrush to add this first color: ACS-12: No. 5.*

23. *Apply another coat this time with a mixture of Reddish-Brown XNAC-47 + Golden Brown XNAC-37.*

24. *The tip of the Horn which is more exposed to the fire launched from the mouth is painted with the No. 4 from the Andrea Color yellow paint set (ACS-11).*

25. *A final glaze with N ° 4 of the Andrea Color red paint set (ACS-04) will unify the shades previously applied.*

26. *We paint the interior of the wings with the airbrush, the light reflection of maximum intensity with a mix of French Orange XNAC-35 + Dark Orange XNAC-36.*

27. *We apply in the same way some shadows accentuating the veins, we use Dark Red XNAC-30.*

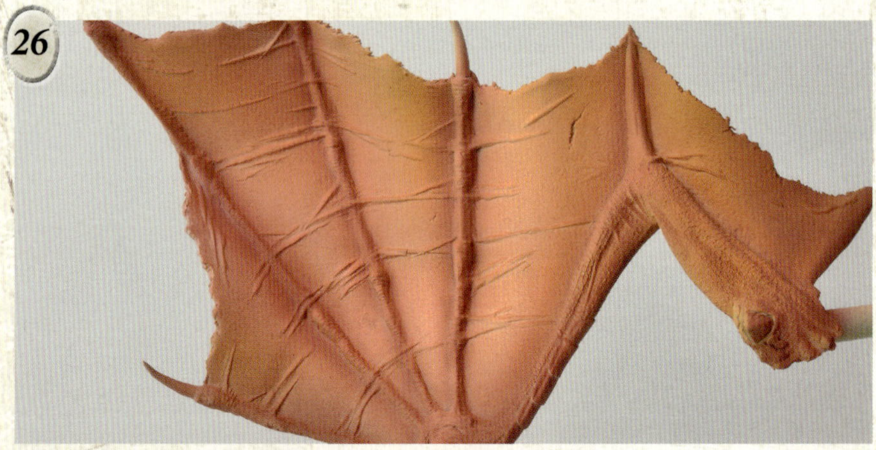

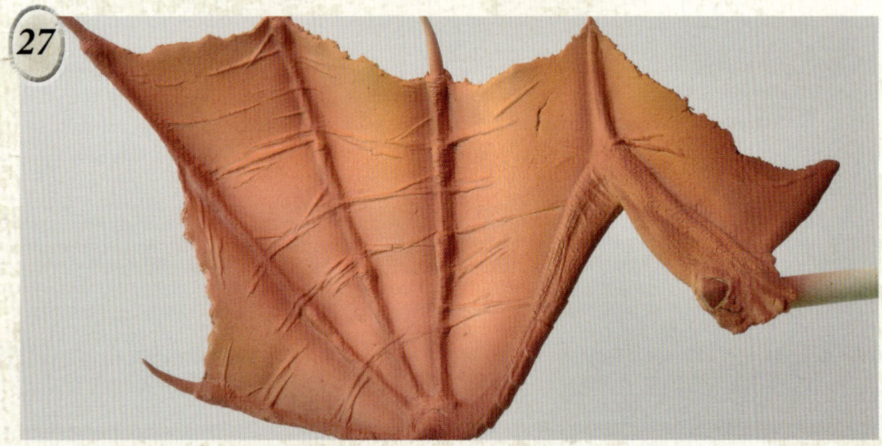

28

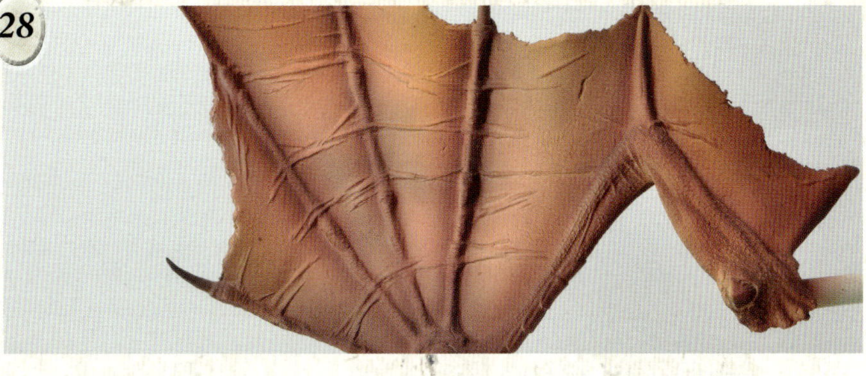

29

30

31

32

28. *We change to the paintbrush to apply various shades of glazes (Navy Blue XNAC-11, Turquoise XNAC-15 and no. 4 of the Andrea Color red paint Set), to do some effects of spots and counter the extreme softness of airbrush.*

29. *As you can see, the top of the wing has been painted in shades of Blue, Green and Very Dull Red, a product of the mixing of Dark Red XNAC-30 + No.5 of the Andrea Color black paint set.*

30. *To highlight the brightness and intensity of the colors on the lower part of the wing, we apply two glazes with the No. 3 and no. 4 of the Andrea Color red paint set.*

31-32. *Finally the finer details like wrinkles, flaking, veins and claws are treated with more attention seeking the most appropriate tone for the highlights and shadows in each case.*

33

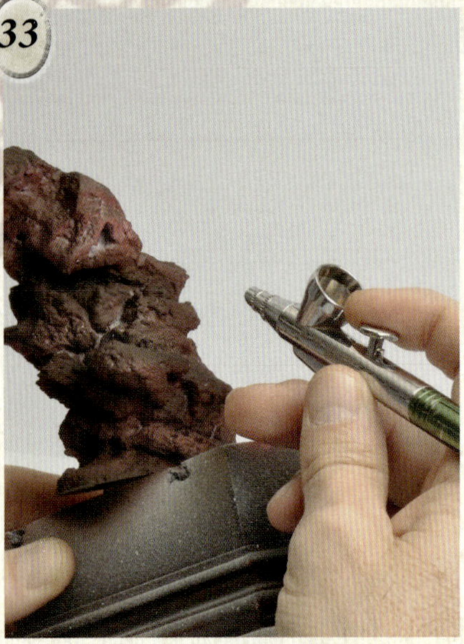

34

35

36

37

38

39

33. *Next we paint the base where the dragon rests. The top is painted with a mixture of Dark Brown Leather XNAC-49 + N ° 6 of the Andrea Color green paint set (ACS-09). At the bottom we will recreate the reflection effect of a lava river, in which the first color we'll apply will be the No. 1 of the Andrea color red paint set.*

34. *We focus on the bottom reinforcing the effect of the light reflection with a dash of the No. 4 of the Andrea Color red paint set.*

35. *On the upper part of the stones, the reflected light is painted with a mixture of N ° 5 + Nº 4 of the Andrea Color NMM paint set (ACS-12).*

36. *We paint the remains of human bones with a paintbrush with a mixture of ochre XNAC-41 + No.5 from the Andrea Color black paint set. Finally, to recreate the same effect of light reflected on these elements use a dash of the No. 4 of the Andrea Color red paint set.*

37. *The base color of the rider´s skin. With this same base color, we paint the other head that is wearing a hood.*

38. *First highlight, several glazes are added with this same mixture to differentiate it from the base color.*

39. *Second tone of highlight. We focus on the same areas that were applied in the previous step.*

40. *With the third highlight center the stroke of the brush only in the points of maximum light.*

41. *First shadow. Being a light skin tone, it will not be necessary to search for another shadow tone. Applying this color with soft glazes, you can get a saturation degree in the facial areas that receive less light.*

42. *The tone of the beard can also serve to shadow the eyes, thus giving a darker aspect to the character.*

40

41

42

3 LIGHT	2 LIGHT	1 LIGHT	BASE COLOR	1 SHADOW	MIDTONE
2 LIGHT + XNAC 01	ACS 01: Nº4 + XNAC 43	BASE + ACS 01: Nº4 XNAC 43	XNAC 01 + XNAC 31 + ACS 01: Nº 4 + ACS 12: Nº 5	BASE + ACS 12: Nº 5	1 SHADOW + XNAC 11

the Warlord

14

Sorondil, Dragon Hunter

WS-30

The last of the legendary hunters has returned. They say that he was seen passing the Frozen Fortress, and some rumors suggest that his objective is in the gorge.

His extinct lineage has hunted and fought all kinds of dragons since the first legends began to be written, and they say that the last dragons have awakened. Sorondil, like the rest of his kind, was born with the oath of hunting engraved on his body and will not rest until his dragon spear passes through the heart of the last of these creatures.

Ithandïr, Blade of Eternity

WS-01 / WSB-01

The two sharp blades stopped suddenly when they were awakened to be gently torn from their scabbards. At his back, the cold wind and the mutilated bodies of his enemies.

The elegant martial skill of Ithandir was only comparable to his legend. Despite his young appearance, few have seen his legendary swords unsheathed and survived to tell about it in the past centuries. As captain of the Edge of Amber, the personal guard of the Empress of the North, it was not usual to witness his illustrious interventions and no one can remember one a failure.

Perhaps now is the time in which someone worthy of a showdown at the height of his skills has been awakened.

Saga gallery

Mad Karnik and Stonebrain Gozbog

WS-09

-"Gozbog!, bring that parchment here in this moment or I will break your head!"

Gozbog did not understand why Karnik always had to yell. He did not understand half of what he said you so Gozbog grabbed the parchment and headed towards his master.

-"And also bring me a little straw!, this spell will require some fire to be effective"

He did not understand why his sullen master was now sending him to the other corner of the cave for straw. A bright idea was coming to life in his tiny and hard brain. This time he would surprise him with his speed and wit and he would surely receive a pair of rats as a reward for dinner.

The image of Gozbog placing the parchment in the chimney was formed in his head until the brutal explosion launched everything through the air. It was the third laboratory that idiot destroyed in the last months, although he had to recognize that their life was much more exciting since he had hired his unpredictable apprentice.

Varathar, Dark Guardian

WSS-01

Varathar is Ithandïr's twin brother and an expert and skilled dragon rider until their extinction. He had an unstoppable overpowering strength riding those gigantic terrestrial reptiles. Not very long ago, Varathar was also the commander of the Guard of the Temple of the Moring. The reason why he abandoned his duties is unknown but rumors are that Zorabeth could have seduced him in some way.

Sulnar, Burning Wing

WS-22

The engraved runes pulsed with the mystical energy that drove them. Sulnar knew at last what they faced and had mobilized the Edge of Amber hoping to stay ahead of events.

He was always one of the most powerful wizards on Earth but his time was approaching and he was conscious of that. Creator of one of the mystical seals that were holding Astaroth, he could feel anxious as he awaited his time for revenge, who was becoming stronger and stronger as the chains holding him lost their power.

All that was left was to hope that soon the, the time to test his skills on the battlefield would come again.

Ainariël Arrow of Light

WS-06

While the elven bow was tightened, Ainariël freed her mind. Little by little she noticed the tension in her arms and back began to disappear. Everything around her became unfocused and smoky in the green shadows of the foliage. Only the tip of her arrow and her attention focused on her goal. That poor unwary had tried to track her down since she entered the jungle

A tenth of a second was enough, an arm slightly showed between a few bushes. He was too careless to be an efficient tracker. The silver arrow flew towards her target with a mortal hiss, Ainariël was already vanished, continuing with the objective that had been entrusted to her by the Edge of Amber.

Daramis, Healing Light

WS-28

The old witch lady prepared her trip with a dark feeling in her heart. The Archmage of the arcane, and only human survivor of the ritual of the seals, was aware of the importance of the situation.

Sulnar, who years ago gave her the spell of youth, had reclaimed it, along with other great lords. Its power allowed her to survive that slaughter, but everything showed that the seals were breaking, and the war was about to begin again.

Zorabeth, Morning Mist
WSS-02

Ithandïr was heading there. The other nine seals had been broken, the ritual performed, and Varathar, the former guardian, had abandoned his post after being seduced by Zwëothel.

This were the terrible news that she had in her head while the skillful rider moved to the general meeting. It had not been few who, in search of the favor of Nalach, had tried to sully the Temple of the Gorge. But none had survived.

Zorabeth had not been assigned as guardian of the fortress of the morning for no reason. Her tactical intelligence, and her lethal Edge of Jade, the sword forged by the ancient elven blacksmiths, became the nearly impregnable wall of the temple.

Urmuth, Scars of War
WS-15

The scars cover Urmuth's body from his bout with Hørthack. Stripped of his Horde, turned into ashes, and with just a dirty group of warriors, he had been forced to sell his skills to survive.

The good thing is that he never lacked of customers that offered good amounts of money for what he did best, killing and sowing fear and bewilderment.

Some time ago, a hooded gentleman offered him the possibility of revenge, promising him a large sum of money and an axe poisoned with the stolen souls of a host of fallen warriors.

Now, Urmuth was waiting impatient near the jungle of Elder, the time to comply with the instructions of the dark rider and recover again the command of a horde which, by nature, belonged to him.

Rhonen, Panther Claws

WS-18

It had been some time since the old Dark Elf Scout, had been sent to the Plains to build relationships with tribal warlords on the other side of the continent.

At the forefront of the clans, Rhonen had been chosen by his skill by Hørthack to pave way for the core of his army by his secrecy and his fierce warriors, experts in the art of the surprise attack and ambush.

Verthandi, Burning Ice

WS-26

Verthandi's reddish hair was almost as well-known as her vehement nature. The female chieftain of the tribe of Vesta, her beauty equaled her ability in combat.

Usual companion of Hørthack, she had become one of the members of his personal guard.

Hørthack "Black Crow"

WS-07

Lord of the Ochre Plains. Hørthack was trained to fight since childhood, like the rest of the men and women from the Golden Plains since immemorial times. After Urmuth's the cruel brutal massacres, he began to join the free tribes one by one. Elevated to Lord of the Clans, Hørthack looked northward, and prepared an army to cross the Jungle of Elder, the natural border that always retained the tribes in the arid plains, in order to claim a better place for its people to settle.

Orog Broken Fang

WS-11

Volgor was one of the most brutal creatures than Orog had seen since his birth. And that was a lot to say. It was a delight to watch his Lord crushing skulls and destroying amours, while his furious figure crossed the battlefield.

His eyes squinted when a small silhouette wrapped in flames appeared on the other side of the river. It was time for him to play. Orog, slowly placed one of his claws into a disgusting bag in his fur cape while he muttered something like some mild gurgling growls, he drop some rune stones soaked in blood.

Immediately, some gray branches began to grow toward one of the goblins who were accompanying him. The unnatural roots surrounded the surprised creature and stretched him with incredible speed launching thronging him into the air. A quizzical smile appeared on Orog's smiled while he was watching the body of his unfortunate companion brutally crashing and enjoying the pleasant crunch of his bones. Like his master, he was not subtle, but his magic had always served in a wild and effective way to the Horde.

Grandar Firebeard

WS-27

For many years Firebeard had been crushing green skins, when he received the news. -"Go, it seems that the old ones have decided to move at last". 97-Yeasr-old, he was aware since childhood, but didn't understand how all the thundering armies of the mountains had not yet moved their asses to end those dirty orcs.

Traditionally, young people were sent for 5 years in small groups to battle out of the Plains, and despite being quite fun, Grandar smiled when thinking about the possible feats that he would tell his children when the hordes of Volgor were annihilated once and for all.

Grandar, filled with euphoria and joy, lifted a huge beer mug enchanted by the thoughts of battles and moments of glory that soon would find him.

Volgor, The Skull Hunter

WS-02

A single grunt ordered his warriors to withdraw. He thought that the enemy skull he was holding in his hands would look very good in his collection. He had fought with value for being just a thin pink-skinned guy, but he would not live much longer to the wounds inflected by their followers while he would tried to reach him.

Volgor, rose to his full stature when the human launched himself towards him with feints and deceptions. He lifted his axe above his head and let his rival drive his sword unsuccessfully into his leather-hard skin. He was not was a warrior of deception and subtleties. The taste of blood overflowed into his mouth, filling him with anger and joy. The clumsy human had made a mistake. The sword, was stuck on him and withdrew slowly from Volgor's barely protected torso, but his axe was already chopping with the strength of a bear, going through his enemies' armor and bones.

The combat had been fact and uneven, and was not very satisfying for him. Volgor pulled the small sword from his enemies' flesh and, with an animal roar, the Hunter of Skulls launched himself into combat without waiting for his own horde, wanting to increase the size of his collection.

Drünegar Runekeeper

WS-03

The runes on his axe had been carved during the last 40 Stone Moons by his most skilled blacksmiths. The stones of the grotto sparkled in a strange way, causing a cold feeling of uneasiness in the old guardian.

Rumors that the Orcs of Volgor were moving eastward had been confirmed and mountains were beginning to resonate with echoes of the past. His family had been dishonored before the agreement, but Volgor had been banished.

Drünegar took his axe from the hands of one of the Rune priests, and placed it on his old anvil. It was time to carve the ancient and powerful Rune of revenge. Only he was allowed to do so, because he was the Rune guardian of the ancient lineage.

The horns of war would sound tomorrow in the thunderous mountains.

Arlith, Silent Shadow

WS-17

The hook was anchored on the roof, and Arlith climbed by rope with the agility and stealth of a shadow. Without noise, and unseen she dropped herself through the window into the inner courtyard.

Once she was in, she got rid of the first guard with a smooth movement. The blade had reached its destination with a deadly precision. A second guard suffered a strike from behind and before he was aware of what was happening, his inert body was on the floor behind the curtains.

Only women could join the assassins of the Arcane clan, since only they had the skills that were necessary for that. The old order did not allow failure and Arlith, the most promising young girl in the last years, went carefully and quietly to the Golden Gate behind which her ultimate goal was waiting. She never failed.

Olfo "Fast Feet"

WS-25

He was almost lucky that a noble who contracted him to plunder that cave of ruffians, refused to pay him what they had previously agreed.

It was not difficult to enter the mansion, and empty the chest of taxes and leave an empty pantry for that cocky jerk.

With a little smile and a full stomach, Olfo took off his red wig, he covered his head with his hood, and began to run to lost himself into the night, leaving behind a detailed note of thanks to his unfortunate but generous patron.

Falkar, Wandering Sword

WS-19

Falkar is one of the most famous "swords for rent" from the frozen reaches. After years of service in the frozen bastion as a Royal Messenger, Falkar knew the roads that crossed the mountains like no one else, and his skill with all kinds of weaponry made him one of the most famous mercenaries in the North of the continent.

White Wolf

WS-21

If you do not have the means to pay Falkar or if your goals are something more sinister, White Wolf is your man, almost as skillful in combat as Falkar but less scrupulous. He was expelled from the Royal Guard of the frozen Bastion before it was disolved.

Rumors talk about murders and conspiracies to achieve positions of power in the old guard, and although they are not proven, White Wolf was part of them all. Cold as ice, nobody expects mercy, or a fair match with this mercenarie.

Brogan, The Bonecrasher

WS-14

Ancient warrior of the Golden order and protector of the Temple of the ancients, Brogan was banished from it many years ago. Nobody except their old masters knew the reason why this quiet mercenary was expelled, and nobody made any questions about it.

Brogan earned his nickname renting his services to the nobles and warlords of the Blood Islands. Currently he was seen on merchant ships traveling towards the old continent. The purposes of these trips are also unknown, but the rumors say that his axe is no longer serving his own affair.

Bestor Savage Claw

WS-20

The Bestor clan is one of the most powerful of the Elder Jungle, but unlike the Dagor, is a nomadic tribe. They are a hunter clan, and move behind their scouts, searching for prey in the contours of the jungle.

Bestor, is one of their most skilled hunters, and one of the few who have traveled on a hunting mission or exploration away from the Green mangroves.

It was said that he was the one who located and organized the hunt that began with the Uru tribe, disappearing until his return to help his people.

Dagor, Ancient Fury

WS-23

Very little is known aboutthe Dagor clan. They are territorial, but they are not used to move further than the northern area of the jungle of Elder.

This ancient creature, has ruled one of the most savage jungles of the entire old continent. It is said that he is wise and tempered and no foreigner dares to bother him without his consent in his domain. His strength is comparable with a demon's one, and his roar is audible from the Golden Plains when directed with vengeful fury at his powerful warriors.

Uru, the Juggernaut

WS-16

These bandits had been easily crushed by Uru. The spectacle of that muscular beast charging against the enemy was something worth seeing. If any survived his first charge, it took little for the warriors of Rhonen to speedily eliminate the battered helpless survivors. Since the Juggernaut joined the tribes of Horthack, the road had become more rapid and safe.

They ignored the reasons that movedthis guttural warrior them, but of course, Horthack knew it was a great help to have him on their side

Luriel, Sacred Fist
WS-13

Rector priest of the Warrior Ring from the Temple of the Ancients, he has devoted his life to hunting and destruction of everything God Menoth, Lord of death, has let slip from its bowels. For Luriel, those returning from the dark side, and those who dare to call them are an affront to those who have not completed their cycle, an abomination that must be remedied.

The last eclipse and the twin moons dyed red augured doors that have been opened. Luriel has taken command of the third ring and has prepared the greatest purification. The hunt has begun, and the natural order of the sacred cycle depends on it.

Leogante, Wings of Redemption
WS-08

After the last eclipse, the third ring made the sacrifice that the ancient redeemers saw as irrefutable proof of unshakeable faith. He had summoned one of the ancients. The pure and devastating power of Leogante was introduced into the empty body and soul of the sacrificed warrior, relocating bone and muscle alike. A destroyer of darkness, a powerful Warrior, called only at the most sinister of times had been reborn.

His bright wings were deployed slowly at the time that his body was changed. The old clergy anointed his body while they opened the coffers with the ancient sacred weapons. A deep voice, as born in the depths of the most ancient mountains resounded in the head of Luriel.

"The hunt has begun, so that the redemption will take us to the last corners of this planet".

Astaroth the Annihilator

WS-12

Nobody talks about Astaroth today. That is because the few who survived him prefer not to mention his name.

Few creatures of this or any other time have brought so much destruction with them. Never before had anything or anyone been delighted in the same way with the most wild and irrational violence. Among his dark brothers, Astaroth is the most skilled in combat and, constantly thirsty for blood. He carries on with fight and destruction leaving desolate fortresses and destroyed cities.

Behind nine magical seals, he was locked up for centuries, buried in the large crack under tons of stone and powerful spells. Now that Nalach has been awakened, the nine seals have become weak and the old seers are beginning to hear his bellows with increasing clarity.

Zwëothel, Queen of Darkness

WS-31

Her sinuous figure shuddered on her throne to think about the past times. Formerly Zwëothel belonged to the Amber Tower, but that was long ago. Equal to Ulnar in skills, he was always too conservative for her .

The rest of the primitive creatures that inhabited the continent could and should have been mastered. Thousands of servants had helped to maintain and increase the greatness of a clearly superior race. But now, centuries after the exile, she had been made stonger, and had created an army of the undead. Nalach would try to use it. Beelphegor was headed to his fortress and Varathar was on his way to meet her.

Well, perhaps everything was not lost for her race. They were simply asleep, and she will be the one who will be able to wake them up...

Menhow, Dark Shadow

WS-10

Dark graves and blemished tombs. Zwëothel had been very busy lately. The old knight began to straighten up. Sinister crunches of his bones and the clashing of his rusty armor could only mean one thing. Dark souls responded with greater ease in the last moons. No better weapon than an ancient warrior, devoid of any guilt or reason.

Death puppets controlled by the one capable of moving the invisible strings. The ancient warrior grabbed his sword, a weapon thirsty for the heat of the living. He was ready to increase the sinister power of his mistress.

Nalach, Evil Shadow

WS-24

Four centuries he has been moving the tabs, and finally all of them had been located where he wanted them to be. His thirst for revenge had been mitigated in recent years, giving way to a fun and seductive destructive anxiety. It was not uncontrolled anger over the pain of the seals, rather it is a relief to think of the fun plans that he had prepared for those who locked him up.

Beelphegor was an intelligent and powerful servant, and finally the rites had been completed. Only nine seals were left to break to release the last of his brothers, and new cards were handed out on the table. It was a good thing is that this time it was he who dealt, and never left anything to chance.

Khaerus The summoner

WS-04

-"With patience you will be a great sorcerer" he was told since he was very young. But patience has never been one of his qualities. His skill in casting spells was innate.

It was always evident that his future was going to be great and that he was going to make history.

All these thoughts were revolving in his head while hi battered and immobile body was floating in that damn Lake of blood. Beelphegor had used him, betraying his trust.

It was history, first Baal, and then Nalach.This was the second time he betrayed him and now, after facing the Harvester, he was broken and humiliated while he was watching that quizzical smile walking away. Well, now the Reaper despised him, and that would be his mistake. If his destiny was to be written, he would be the one writing it. He will survive to amend his mistakes. He let his eyes close and murmured a few words which would surely not be his last spell.

Beelphegor, The Soul Reaper

WS-05

A crooked smile showed under the sinister hood, Nalach had emerged from the spring of blood that poured during the latest moons. The ritual had been completed and its ancient sword had drunk hundreds of souls.

He was more awake than ever, eager as always for the sensations that only death could provide, but with the certainty that soon the events would turn the course of history forever.

Beelphegor, freed at last from any hint of his former conscience, turned away from that cursed spring with the slowness of one who knows that his destiny has already been written.